BATTLE PRAYERS
&
DECLARATIONS

For

YOUR FAMILY

Freda Lade-Ajugbi x

05/11/2022

ALSO BY FREDA LADE-AJUMOBI

Prayer For Today - *(An Inspirational Book of Encouragement and Prayers)*

BATTLE PRAYERS
& Declarations

For

YOUR FAMILY

52 Week Scripture, Devotional

& Guided Prayer Book for Praying Parents®

FREDA LADE-AJUMOBI

BATTLE PRAYERS & DECLARATONS FOR YOUR FAMILY

Copyright © 2022 Freda Lade-Ajumobi

All Rights Reserved

ISBN-13 : 9798355979836

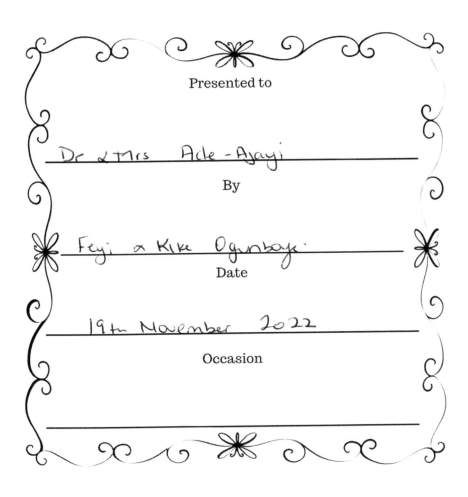

Presented to

Dr & Mrs   Ade - Ajayi

By

Feyi   & Kike   Ogunboye.

Date

19th November   2022

Occasion

DEDICATION

I dedicate this book to our Heavenly Father, my Lord and Saviour, Jesus Christ and the Holy Spirit. You are my inspiration!

To you Praying Parents.

I prayed diligently for you and your precious children as I wrote this book, and the Lord gave me a word for you in:

2 Chronicles 7:16

"For now I have chosen and sanctified this house, that My name may be there forever; and My eyes and My heart will be there perpetually."

CONTENTS

ACKNOWLEDGMENTS

I want to acknowledge and express my gratitude to the following people who have had an impact on my life:

I am eternally grateful to our Lord and Saviour, Jesus Christ, who made the impossible possible through His shed blood on Calvary. You are truly incredible!

My darling husband, Afolabi, and son, Timi. Thank you for being there. I will forever be grateful to the Lord for you.

To my siblings, thank you for your love and support.

In loving memory of my dear parents, Mr & Mrs Mojola who are now at rest in the Lord. The legacy continues.

To my Church family, Church of New Destiny, Praying Parents, Warriors of God, Destiny Changers and all my encouragers, I am truly grateful.

Holy Spirit, my teacher, comforter and friend, thank you!

INTRODUCTION

God's Word repeatedly tells us that our words have incredible power. In any given situation, the words we speak have the power to give life to our children and grandchildren. We can use them to bring life and blessings, or we can use them to bring curses and death. *"Death and life are in the power of the tongue, And those who love it will eat its fruit." – Proverbs 18:21*

One day, the Lord said to me, "Don't leave your family to chance. If you are not praying and fasting for your family, you are leaving your family to chance, and anything can happen. Don't put the blame on me if something bad occurs. I have provided you with every resource necessary." Before God spoke those words to me, I had been praying vague prayers like "Lord, bless me and bless my family" without a specific biblical reference. Hearing God speak to me made me realise I wasn't speaking the Word of God into existence. I wasn't putting much thought and effort into the words I spoke over my family. So, when I asked the Lord to instruct me on how to pray and confess His Word, He began teaching me to be prudent and guard my tongue. He taught me to choose my words intentionally by speaking and praying His life-giving truths over my family. As I began to read the Bible and meditate on the Word, it made me feel like the Apostle Peter, that *"You [alone] have the words of eternal life [you are our only hope]."* *– John 6:68*

Using the Word of God in prayer is the key to answered prayer – prayer that brings results. The Word and the Spirit are one; they are not apart from each other. The Word of God is of the Spirit of God. When we apply the Word personally to ourselves and our family, it makes contact with Jesus, the Living Word, and sets His spiritual laws into motion; and we shall be of those whom Isaiah says, *"Shall build the old waste places; You shall raise up the foundations of many generations; And you shall be called the Repairer of the Breach, The Restorer of Streets to Dwell In."* *(Isaiah 58:12)*

As Christian parents, we have the amazing privilege that God has bestowed upon us to speak words of life over our children. Our words matter. We can use it to encourage or deter, to lift them or bring them down. When you use BATTLE PRAYERS & DECLARATIONS FOR YOUR FAMILY as a weekly devotional to pray for your family, you strengthen them through the anointing and power of the Holy Spirit, which lifts them higher and helps them become stronger.

Many parents struggle with prayer. Some parents don't know how to pray about specific challenges they are facing in their family and have become discouraged in prayer. BATTLE PRAYERS & DECLARATIONS FOR YOUR FAMILY will help you to pray prayers that bring results. The Bible instructs us in Job 22:28 to *"...declare a thing, and it will be established for you; so light will shine on your ways."* This scripture is a powerful testament to the power of spoken words. When we decree and declare according to God's Word, we operate in our dominion authority and activate the power to establish God's will in our family.

God has not only given us His Word, but He has also given us the

Holy Spirit to help our weakness when we don't know how to pray as we ought. *"Likewise the Spirit also helps in our weaknesses. For we do not know what we should pray for as we ought, but the Spirit Himself makes intercession for us with groanings which cannot be uttered. Now He who searches the hearts knows what the mind of the Spirit is, because He makes intercession for the saints according to the will of God"* (Romans 8:26-27).

The words we speak are not vain; they are Spirit and life, mighty through God to the pulling down of strongholds.

It is also important not just to pray, but to fast and pray. The Bible states the great things that will happen when we fast and pray for our children. *"Is this not the fast that I have chosen: To loose the bonds of wickedness, to undo the heavy burdens, to let the oppressed go free, and that you break every yoke?"* (Isaiah 58:6)

Great blessings flow from fasting and praying for our children. It produces great results, and extraordinary things begin to happen. The Bible states that when we fast in God's chosen way, *"Then your light shall break forth like the morning, Your healing shall spring forth speedily, And your righteousness shall go before you; The glory of the Lord shall be your rear guard. Then you shall call, and the Lord will answer; You shall cry, and He will say, 'Here I am.'* (Isaiah 58:8-9)

When we stand in the gap by making intercession, fasting, praying and battling for the lives and destinies of our children, it results in the following:

- **"Then your light shall break forth like the morning"** *(The Light of Christ will fill your home, your children and your family. The darkness in your children's lives and your home will dissipate).*

- **"Your healing shall spring forth speedily"** *(Physical, spiritual and emotional health will return to you and your family quickly).*

- **"And your righteousness shall go before you"** *(Your righteousness before God and man will be visibly seen. It will make way for you and your children and protect you).*

- **"The glory of the Lord shall be your rear guard"** *(The glorious power of God and the Lord Jesus Christ will protect and defend your family. You will have spiritual protection on every side).*

- **"Then you shall call, and the Lord will answer"** *(The Lord will hear and answer your prayers for your family; and plentifully bestow His favour on your home, so that you will have no reason to complain).*

- **"You shall cry, and He will say, 'Here I am.'** *(He will immediately appear to bring help and relief. You shall have His presence with you to comfort and refresh, to help and supply, to protect and defend your family).*

Fervent prayers coupled with fasting from time to time infuse us with the power to draw our children back home, and no matter what challenges they face, their story will be like that of the prodigal son; it will end in praise! Our children's lives would be full of light, full of healing, full of righteousness and full of the glory of the LORD!

Isaiah was writing to the family of Israel when he counselled them in Isaiah 58:7, *"When you see the naked, that you cover him, and not to hide yourself from [the needs of] your own flesh and blood?"* *(AMP)*. We could interpret this verse as saying that we should love our children, cover them in prayer and fast for them. In the same way we expect our heavenly Father to stand by us in all circumstances, we also ought to stand by our children despite their waywardness. God expects us to stand in the place of prayer, fighting for our children's lives and destinies, and *"You shall cry, and He will say, 'Here I am.'."*.

We serve a God who watches over our children and listens to us when we call out to Him. When we pray, He hears us. When we cry to Him and present our children's case in the courts of heaven, the Lord will answer and rescue them from the traps of the enemy. God doesn't expect you to be a perfect parent, but He does want you to be a praying parent. No one in the Bible was perfect.

Praying for our families empowers us to repair anything that has torn the relationship apart. We gain the power to repair generational family problems, restore unity, maintain family bonds in the Lord, and leave a spiritual inheritance of love that can last for generations. Through the power of prayer, we sanctify ourselves to become what Isaiah calls *"the repairer of the breach."* By the anointing and power of the Holy Spirit, and in the name of Jesus, we can stop the generational flow of affliction which plagues our families from generation to generation. In the place of prayer, we can fill the void left by a previous generation and raise new foundations for the next generation, therefore "repairing the breach" and breaking the yoke of the past. *"Those from among you shall build the old waste places; you shall raise up the foundations of many generations; and you shall be called the Repairer of the Breach, the Restorer of Streets to Dwell In."* (Isaiah 58:12)

How do we pray for our children and families?

For prayers to bring results, they must be based on God's Word. They must not be religious prayers that have no power; they must be effective, accurate and bring results. Prayer is that Word of God that comes alive in our mouths. *"But what does it say? "The word is near you, in your mouth and in your heart"* (Romans 10:8). This is the Word of faith. God watches over His Word to bring it to pass. Are you ready to speak the Word over your family? God is ready to perform it! "Then the Lord said to me, *"You have seen well, for I am ready to perform My word"* (Jer 1:12).

As a Praying Parent, you are called to be a prayer warrior, an intercessor, seeking the face of the Lord, inquiring, listening to the voice of the Holy Spirit, meditating and loving God as your first priority. You are called to be a man of prayer (praying father), and a woman of prayer (praying mother). You are Praying Parents. You are the righteousness of God in Christ Jesus. Your prayers will bring healing, deliverance, salvation and prosperity to your children and usher in God's next move into your home and family life.

BATTLE PRAYERS & DECLARATIONS FOR YOUR FAMILY combines prayer and confession of the Word of God to bring life-transforming change into your life and your home. Whenever you go through adverse circumstances with your child, speak these prayers and declarations over him/her.

Prayer and confession of scriptural prayers is a very effective weapon of war, and it is what led me out of darkness and into the light I now experience. Prayer and speaking the Word of God have power! It worked for me, rescued me from a pit of despair, and gave me the strength to face each new day. It gave me hope where I didn't know where to turn, bringing healing into my life. I know it will work for you, it will work for your children, it will work for your family. You can use BATTLE PRAYERS & DECLARATIONS FOR YOUR FAMILY as a weekly devotional or buy them as a gift for friends and family.

Each prayer is written with your child in mind, to inspire, motivate and encourage you to pray for your children. You can use BATTLE PRAYERS & DECLARATIONS FOR YOUR FAMILY to pray for yourself and others. Read, meditate and confess the prayers. Praying God's Word brings results, for the Word is of the Spirit of God.

These prayers were written under the inspiration of the Holy Spirit and are based on the Word of God. God will not turn away your prayer; our God hears and answers prayers. He is near to all who call on Him. "Now this is the confidence that we have in Him, that if we ask anything according to His will, He hears us. And if we know that He hears us, whatever we ask, we know that we have the petitions that we have asked of Him." (1 John 5:14-15) Read BATTLE PRAYERS & DECLARATIONS FOR YOUR FAMILY and speak the confessions every day for the whole week. You can use it as intercessory prayers for others by praying it in the third person.

Most of the prayers have scripture references. Prayer that yields results must be based on God's Word. "For the Word of God is living and powerful, and sharper than any two-edged sword, piercing even to the division of soul and spirit, and of joints and marrow, and is a discerner of the thoughts and intents of the heart." (Hebrews 4:12) These are prayers that bring light and hope.

If you are going through difficult times, I encourage you not to give up. There is light at the end of the tunnel.

Speak the prayer declarations each day of the week. God bless you as you commit to prayer and fellowship with Him by using BATTLE PRAYERS & DECLARATIONS FOR YOUR FAMILY as a weekly devotional.

A WORD FROM THE LORD

Dear Praying Parent,

Thus says the Lord, "The mighty things I am about to do in your children's lives are beyond your expectations. I have heard your prayers, I have seen your tears. There is a rising and a lifting up. Therefore you must rejoice. Your souls have escaped the wrath of the enemy. The cords and snares are broken, I have lifted your burdens. The evil yokes that held your family bound are broken, destroyed! I have not given your children as prey to the enemy. The enemy's teeth are broken!

"I broke the fangs of the wicked,
And plucked the victim from his teeth."
(Job 29:17)

I am taking your children into higher dimensions of My glory. Things you have not known will begin to unfold before you. Your children will start to see things anew, afresh, because I have given them a fresh anointing.

"But my horn [my emblem of strength and power] You have exalted like that of a wild ox; I am anointed with fresh oil [for Your service].
(Psalm 92:10) AMP

My love for your family is a blanket all around and over you. I love your family with My everlasting love. I am preserving your children for My glory. They are the apple of my eye and the treasure in My heart, my special possession.

"But you are A CHOSEN RACE, A royal PRIESTHOOD, A CONSECRATED NATION, A [special] PEOPLE FOR God's OWN POSSESSION, so that you may proclaim the excellencies [the wonderful deeds and virtues and perfections] of Him who called you out of darkness into His marvellous light. Once you were NOT A PEOPLE [at all], but now you are GOD'S PEOPLE; once you had NOT RECEIVED MERCY, but now you have RECEIVED MERCY."

(1 Peter 2:9-10)

My passion for dying at the cross came because of My everlasting love for you and your family. I died so your family might be set free. I purchased your freedom and broke the chains that bound you. I took your troubles and brought you My Peace. Lean on me at all times and talk to me about everything. Let me know how you are feeling. I am here for you. I hear your thoughts, and I know your heart. You are precious to Me. I am your Keeper, your shade at your right hand. I will not allow the sun to strike your family by day nor the moon by night. I am your Keeper, the pillar that holds your lives together.

Peace be upon you. My Peace is here for you. Receive My Peace. My Peace is within your walls and prosperity within your palaces (Ps. 122:7). Peace be within your children. Peace be within your home. Peace within your job and your business. As the mountains surround Jerusalem, so do I surround you and your children from this time forth and forever (Ps. 125:2). The sceptre of wickedness I will not allow to rest on your family, for you are precious in My sight.

Lift up your eyes! Lift up your head! Your time of rising is here! I will not allow your foot to be moved. Your help has come. I have made your family a flame of fire. A burning flame whose light cannot be put out. You are light in the midst of darkness. Your children are light. Their light will not dim.

I rejoice over your family because you are all beautiful, the work of My hands, and I am proud of you always. I will permit no one to do you wrong. I rebuke kings for your sake. I will say to them, "Do not touch My anointed ones and do My prophets no harm" (Ps. 105:14). I will satisfy your family with the bread of heaven. Water will gush out of the rock for you, running in your dry places like a river. I will bring you out with joy, and you, My chosen ones, with gladness. You and your children will inherit the labour of the nations. I have delivered you out of your distress and will lead you the right way. I sent My Word and healed you and your children. Hold on to My Word; it brings healing to the soul, the mind and the spirit.

I have delivered your family from destruction. I have redeemed you out of the hand of the enemy. From everlasting to everlasting, I remain your God, the Holy One of Israel, the Ancient of Days. I will not break my covenant concerning you and your family, nor will I alter the Word that has gone out of My mouth, for I have magnified My Word above all My name (Ps. 138:2). You are blessed. My faithfulness and My mercy shall be with you and your children, and in My name your horn shall be exalted (Ps. 89:24). The enemy shall not outwit your children, nor the son of wickedness afflict your family. I will beat down your enemies before your face, and plague those who hate you and your children. (Ps. 89:22-23)

My faithfulness and My mercy shall be with you and your family now and forever, and in My name your horn shall be exalted (Ps.

89:24). My Presence will be with you and I will give you rest."

Says the Lord of Hosts, your Redeemer, the Holy One of Israel.

DECLARATIONS OF GRATITUDE & THANKSGIVING

David was once a shepherd boy who became the king of Israel. While instructing and guiding the sheep, he was lowly and lonely. He was pushed to the rear of the crowd, where no one acknowledged or even looked at him. His voice was muffled and ignored by men, but he used it in praising God and soon wrote 73 out of the total 150 Psalms. David wrote many Psalms of praise and thanksgiving and frequently declared his trust in the Lord despite his circumstances. He was courageous, committed and praised God in his wilderness season. Whilst Goliath scoffed at the God of Israel, David trusted the God of his fathers. He changed his story with thanksgiving to God and became one of the greatest kings on earth. David never stopped thanking God for his past and present existence. He never forgot his humble beginnings.

As parents, we need to thank God in all circumstances because God calls us to live a life of gratitude. We must give thanks since it is God's will. If you are in a lowly state like king David, praise God that those bad events do not control you. The more we thank God, the more we see Him, and the darkness fades away. As you express thanks, the Lord will extend His hand to protect you and your family from the vengeance of your foes. (Ps. 138:7). And when you're on a higher level, thank and praise Him as well. Appreciate God for who He is in your children's lives. Thank Him for what he has done for you and your family. Appreciate Him with songs and praises, with psalms and hymns.

Today, you and your family are in the land of the living and not in the land of the dead; let us give Him thanks and praise! Let us thank God in every situation. *"Do not be anxious about anything, but in every situation, by prayer and petition, with thanksgiving, present your requests to God. And the peace of God, which surpasses all understanding, will guard your hearts and minds through Christ Jesus" (Phil. 4:6-7).*

Words of Wisdom: God continues to provide for our families through His constant love and tender mercies. He protects our children in their going out and coming in. He leads us in the paths of righteousness for His name's sake. David was able to defeat Goliath thanks to the God of Israel. This same God is with you and your children today. With God's love and tender mercies over your family and His breath in your lungs, I encourage you to give Him thanks in all things.

Scripture Meditation: 1 Thessalonians 5:16-18 (AMP)
"Rejoice always and delight in your faith; be unceasing and persistent in prayer; in every situation [no matter what the circumstances] be thankful and continually give thanks to God; for this is the will of God for you in Christ Jesus."

Your Declaration: Lord, I never fail to remember how you have rescued my family. I offer you a sacrifice of praise and thanksgiving because you have saved the souls of my children from the valley of the shadow of death, our eyes from tears, and our feet from falling. I praise you, for you have answered me and have become my salvation (Ps. 118:21). I am grateful that you hear and respond to my requests. I thank you for you are good! Your mercy endures forever (Ps. 118:1). Because you have answered me, I shall continue to call on you as long as I live. O Lord my God, you are very great: you are clothed with honour and majesty, you cover yourself with light as with a garment, you stretch out the heavens like a curtain (Ps. 104:1-2). May your glory endure forever. I thank you as I remember the marvellous works you have done for our family. You fight our battles and give us victory above all others. You have shown us your mercy, and your goodness has carried us through these many years. I give thanks to you, for you are good! Your mercy endures forever. I appreciate your kindness and amazing work for us. May the Lord God of Israel be praised from the beginning to the end! In the name of Jesus, I say, "Amen!" This is my prayer and declaration in Jesus' name.

PRAY FOR CHILDREN OF THE WORLD:
Pray that God will raise warriors in them.
He will provide for them through His love and tender mercies.

- WEEK 2 –

DECLARATIONS FOR SUCCESS

After reading the story of Joseph in Genesis 39, it leaves me with a clear impression, he was diligent, hardworking and gave his best in everything. Despite adversity, Joseph proved to be a success story from the moment he came to Egypt. He was sold by his jealous brothers at the young age of 17 to the Ishmaelites, who then sold him to Egypt, where he was so far away from home and family. With nothing and no experience whatsoever in the vocation of a servant, Joseph defied all odds and succeeded in everything he did as he served in the home of his Egyptian master. His response is remarkable given the circumstances. He could have succumbed to depression due to his brother's intense hostility and rejection of him and his current circumstances in Egypt. But he did not lose hope or courage. Instead, he worked with all his heart as working for the Lord.

"The LORD was with Joseph, so he succeeded..." (Gen 39:2). All he had was the Lord, which is all he needed to be successful.

Words of Wisdom: It takes the Lord to make a man successful, wherever he may be. When our children live with God as the Lord, whether they are in prison or the penthouse, the pedestal, or the pit, what matters is that they live their lives in and through the Lord. So, I encourage you not to despise the day of small beginnings. It results in great blessings in the long run.

Scripture Meditation: Genesis 39:2-6 (AMP)

"The Lord was with Joseph, and he [even though a slave] became a successful and prosperous man; and he was in the house of his master, the Egyptian. Now his master saw that the Lord was with him and that the Lord caused all that he did to prosper (succeed) in his hand. So Joseph pleased Potiphar and found favour in his sight and he served him as his personal servant. He made Joseph overseer over his house, and he put all that he owned in Joseph's charge. It happened that from the time that he made Joseph overseer in his house and [put him in charge] over all that he owned, that the Lord blessed the Egyptian's house because of Joseph; so the Lord's blessing was on everything that Potiphar owned, in the house and in the field. So Potiphar left all that he owned in Joseph's charge; and with Joseph there he did not [need to] pay attention to anything except the food he ate."

Your Declaration: I declare that my children are consistent and hardworking. The Lord's blessing brings prosperity and abundance into their lives. They are diligent and not lazy. They are a success and not a failure. God helps my children as they work hard and are persistent with their goals. The Lord takes pleasure in their prosperity. My children's souls shall be made rich. They shall eat in plenty and be satisfied and praise the name of the Lord our God. They shall never be put to shame (Joel. 2:26). In everything, they have great success because the Lord is with them (1 Sam. 18:14). They can do all things through Christ who strengthens them (Phil. 4:13). The Book of God's Law shall not depart from their mouth, but they shall read and meditate on it day and night, so that they may be careful to do everything by following all that is written in it; for then they will make their way prosperous and will be successful (Josh.1:8). With God, nothing is or shall ever be impossible for my children (Luke 1:37). They will find favour and success in the sight of God and man (Prov. 3:4). This is my prayer and declaration in Jesus' name.

PRAY FOR CHILDREN OF THE WORLD:
Pray the Lord will be with them and make them
prosperous and successful.

- WEEK 3 -

DECLARATIONS
FOR DIVINE FAVOUR

In the story of Esther, when King Ahasuerus was looking for a new queen, all the beautiful young women in the land were brought into the palace. They were given the opportunity to adorn themselves with all the beauty preparations before they were brought for an audience with the king. The young woman who is able to win the king's favour and become his favourite will succeed Vashti as queen. All the other women grabbed the best items to beautify themselves, but when the turn came for Esther to go in to see the king, she "requested nothing except what Hegai the king's eunuch and assistant who was in charge of the women, advised." The result was that Esther obtained favour! *"And Esther found favour in the sight of all who saw her." (Esther 2: 15)*

"The king loved Esther more than all the other women, and she obtained grace and favour in his sight more than all the virgins; so he set the royal crown upon her head and made her queen instead of Vashti. Then the king made a great feast, the Feast of Esther, for all his officials and servants; and he proclaimed a holiday in the provinces and gave gifts according to the generosity of a king." (Esther 2: 17-18)

Words of Wisdom: When you are entirely dependent on the Lord's unmerited favour, you are trusting Him and in a position of rest. You will not have to struggle; your children will not have to struggle. God gives unmerited favour to the humble. When you depend on Jesus alone, the Lord Himself will increase and bless you. Like Esther, you and your children will stand out in a crowd and obtain grace and favour with God and man.

Scripture Meditation: 1 Peter 5: 6-7 (AMP)

"Therefore humble yourselves under the mighty hand of God [set aside self-righteous pride], so that He may exalt you [to a place of honour in His service] at the appropriate time, casting all your cares [all your anxieties, all your worries, and all your concerns, once and for all] on Him, for He cares about you [with deepest affection, and watches over you very carefully]."

Your Declaration: I declare that this is my children's set time for favour (Ps. 102:13). God's favour is upon their lives as a cloud of the latter rain (Prov. 16:15). God's favour brings promotion and causes them to increase on every side. He has granted them life and favour, and His divine care has preserved their spirit (Job 10:12). My children will never be without God's favour. They are the object of God's affection. God's favour surrounds them everywhere they go and in everything they do. They are blessed and highly favoured (Luke 1:28). They will be in the right place at the right time. People will go out of their way to be good to my children because God's favour surrounds them. God will do something marvellous in my children at which both ears of everyone who hears it will tingle (1 Sam. 3:11). Because of God's favour, my children's enemies cannot triumph over them. They win battles they don't even have to fight because God fights for them. Their enemies cannot triumph because the Lord has favoured them (Psalm 41:11). My children are satisfied with favour and filled with God's blessing. They possess the west and the south (Deut. 33:23). They receive God's extraordinary favour. This is my prayer and declaration in Jesus' name.

PRAY FOR CHILDREN OF THE WORLD:

Pray they will obtain grace and favour with God and man.

DECLARATIONS
FOR OPEN DOORS

In the Book of Acts 16:23-24, Philippian magistrates arrested Paul and Silas and had them beaten for spreading the news about Jesus. The two are chained in a cell, praying and singing to God. "But about midnight when Paul and Silas were praying and singing hymns of praise to God, and the prisoners were listening to them; suddenly there was a great earthquake, so [powerful] that the very foundations of the prison were shaken and at once all the doors were opened and everyone's chains were unfastened" (Acts 16:25-26). An earthquake shakes the prison, releasing all the doors and chains.

Although Paul and Silas were arrested, beaten, and imprisoned for doing good, they were filled with joy and sang praises to God. Nothing would make them stop praising God. Their singing and praising caused something supernatural to happen. *"...suddenly there was a great earthquake."* This earthquake was so powerful and supernatural that all the doors were opened, and everyone's chains were loosed. Our awesome God provided a miraculous breakthrough for them! He broke the chains that held them bound and opened their prison doors. Chains fell off their feet! Hallelujah! The same God who set Paul and Silas free will open doors for you and your children. Keep praying and singing hymns of praise to Him, and the God of open doors will break through for you in Jesus mighty name.

Words of Wisdom: I encourage you not to lose hope in your children when you experience failures or betrayal. Don't give up; keep praying and singing hymns of praise, and God will open doors for you and your family that no man can shut. The earth will quake and chains of bondage will break! Paul and Silas didn't know how the doors would open, but they knew the awesome God that opens doors.

Scripture Meditation: 2 Samuel 5: 20 (AMP)

"So David came to Baal-perazim, and he defeated them there, and said, "The Lord has broken through my enemies before me, like a breakthrough of water." So he named that place Baal-perazim (master of breakthroughs)."

Your Declaration: I declare doors of testimony, rejoicing and celebrations are open to my family. Doors of breakthrough are open unto my children. God has set before us open doors that no one can shut (Rev. 3:8). We can do all things through Christ who strengthens us (Phil. 4:13). Blocked doors are open; heaven is open, the door of grace and favour is open, financial doors are open. Our gates shall be open continually, they will never shut day or night, so that people may bring us the wealth of the nations (Isa. 60:11). I speak Ezekiel 34:26 that the Lord will make my children and the places around them a blessing. He will make showers come down in their season; there shall be showers of abundant blessing (divine favour) over my children in the name of Jesus. No one will shut the doors that God has opened, and the doors He has closed, no one will open. God has opened tremendous and mighty doors. He has provided miraculous breakthroughs. The door of destruction is closed; hopelessness is closed; affliction is closed; oppression, wickedness and witchcraft are closed. I plead the blood of Jesus on doors of entry into our lives. We are delivered from doors of hell and destruction. We are crowned with God's loving kindness and tender mercies (Ps. 103:4). The Lord has broken through our enemies before us, like a breakthrough of water – we call it our *"Baal Perazim"* (2 Sam. 5:20). This is my prayer and declaration in Jesus' name.

PRAY FOR CHILDREN OF THE WORLD:

That God will open miraculous doors of breakthrough; and deliver them from gates of hell and destruction.

DECLARATIONS FOR PROMOTION

"For promotion cometh neither from the east, nor from the west, nor from the south" (Ps. 75:6 - KJV).

Divine promotion is supernatural. God is our source of promotion. Any promotion man gives is temporary and can be taken away, but the promotion God gives will last and cannot be taken away. Our promotion comes in God's time and way. His love for your family is not based on performances, it is based on His mercy and love. Therefore, your promotion is not natural, it is supernatural.

Hannah declared in 1 Samuel 2:8-9 (ESV), *"He raises up the poor from the dust; he lifts the needy from the ash heap to make them sit with princes and inherit a seat of honour. For the pillars of the earth are the Lord's, and on them he has set the world. He will guard the feet of his faithful ones, but the wicked shall be cut off in darkness, for not by might shall a man prevail."*

Do you have a child who seems to have been on an "ash heap" recently? That child is in the right place for a miracle! God is about to promote and make your child "sit with princes and inherit a seat of honour." If it is you who's been on the "ash heap", it is your set time for promotion. God is turning things around and working it in your favour! You are being set up for a miracle and nothing will stand in God's way of promoting you and your family. Praise God! You have been rightly positioned for a miracle. If you are feeling let down, be encouraged. You and your family are always on God's agenda and no man can reverse the blessing of God on your lives. I pray that your story will be like that of Mordecai in the Book of Esther. He had quick advancement and was divinely promoted in the face of great opposition. This will be your story in Jesus name. God is turning your persecution into promotion. Say, "Hallelujah, thank you Jesus!

Words of Wisdom: Promotion does not come from man but from God. No power can stop the hand of God upon your children's lives. Therefore, any promotion God gives your family will last. Mordecai worshipped God and refused to bow down to Haman. Haman represents your "ash heap". You must refuse to bow down. Don't give up, keep thanking God in the face of opposition and what the enemy means for evil will turn around for your good. There is a rising up for you and your children in the name of Jesus.

Scripture Meditation: Genesis 12:2 - AMP
"And I will make you a great nation, And I will bless you [abundantly], and make your name great (exalted, distinguished); and you shall be a blessing [a source of great good to others]."

Your Declaration: I declare that my children are set up for greatness, breakthrough, and divine upliftment. This is my family's set time of supernatural divine promotion. There is a rising in my family. We are carriers of God's blessings and favour.

We increase with the increase of God (Col. 2:19). We receive promotion and elevation in all our endeavours. The Lord will use His mighty hand of promotion to move my family to the next level in the name of Jesus. My children and I will be remembered and honoured like Mordecai; we will be elevated from the low status of a servant to that of a leader in the name of Jesus (Esther 6:10-11). My children flourish like a palm tree and grow like a cedar in Lebanon (Ps. 92:12). They advance from a lower level to a higher level. The Lord will make them the head (leader) and not the tail (follower), and they will be above only, and will not be beneath (Deut. 28:13). My children's name will be made great so that they can be a blessing to others. God is the Author of my family's divine promotion. We will not be demoted. Though our beginning was small, our latter days will be very great (Job 8:7). This is my prayer and declaration in Jesus' name.

PRAY FOR CHILDREN OF THE WORLD:

Pray that God will make their name great so they will be a blessing to the world.

DECLARATIONS
FOR BUSINESS SUCCESS

The Proverbs 31 woman is undoubtedly an inspiration for aspiring entrepreneurs today. Not only is her home impeccable and organised, but she considers a field and buys it, and from her profits, she plants a vineyard (Prov. 31:16). She has an entrepreneurial spirit about her. She makes linen garments, sells them, and supplies sashes for the merchants (Prov. 31:24). She does not eat the bread of idleness. She is a savvy businesswoman! She sees that her trading is profitable, and her lamp does not go out at night (Prov. 31:18). This woman is a planting of the Lord. She is a tree of righteousness! She makes sound business decisions, is financially responsible and diligent. I pray the Lord will teach your children awesome things in business in the name of Jesus.

Words of Wisdom: The Proverbs 31 woman was a doer, not a dreamer. She watched over the ways of her household. She was a good reflection on her children. An excellent example to follow. The source of her success and competence is revealed in Proverbs 31:30, *"...But a woman who fears the LORD, she shall be praised."* She was deeply dependent on God as her daily source of grace. It is a source available to us and our children. She is full of wisdom because she puts into practice *Proverbs 9:10, "The [reverent] fear of the Lord [that is, worshiping Him and regarding Him as truly awesome] is the beginning and the preeminent part of wisdom [its* *starting point and its essence], And the knowledge of the Holy One is understanding and spiritual insight." (AMP)*

Without Jesus, nothing is worthy of praise. Parents are the ultimate role models for children. No other outside force has a more significant influence. This is why in Proverbs 31:28, *"Her children rise up and call her blessed."* The children are our future, and we must teach them to lead the way. They shall call you "blessed" in Jesus name.

Scripture Meditation: Prov. 2:6 (AMP)
"For the Lord gives [skillful and godly] wisdom; from His mouth come knowledge and understanding.

Your Declaration: I declare the Lord will give my children the treasures of darkness and hidden riches of secret places (Isa. 45:3). God's right hand shall teach my children awesome things in their business (Ps. 45:4). I claim business success for my family today and all year through. We make wise business decisions guided by the Holy Spirit. My children are strong and courageous, not terrified or discouraged in the world of business (Joshua 1:9). They are blessed with creative ideas. The Lord will command the blessing upon their business, and in all that they put their hand to (Deut. 28:8). I plead the blood of Jesus on my family's business and on all that belongs to us. We walk out of the realm of failure into the arena of success. There are increased sales and expanded markets with continuous increase in customers throughout the year, resulting in constant business growth for me and my children. We have favour with our clients. My family's business makes a profit and continues to thrive and prosper. We shall be like a tree planted by the rivers of water, that brings forth its fruit in its season, whose leaf also shall not wither; and whatever we do shall prosper (Ps. 1:3). No weapon formed against me and my children's business shall prosper, and every tongue which rises against us in judgement I condemn in the name of Jesus (Isa. 54:17). I speak blessings, prosperity, success, and fruitfulness into our business affairs. There is promotion and expansion. Our family business will not encounter misfortune or unfavourable circumstances. I break all curses of business failure and sudden collapse. The blessing of the Lord upon my family's business makes us rich. God's blessings bring wealth into my family, and He adds no sorrow or stress to it. (Prov. 10:22). We prosper in all in our business affairs. This is my prayer and declaration in Jesus' name.

PRAY FOR CHILDREN OF THE WORLD:
That God will bless them with great business ideas that will change the world.

- WEEK 7 –

DECLARATIONS
FOR ABUNDANT BLESSINGS

Our words have a powerful impact on the lives of people around us, and spoken blessings can provide hope, encouragement, and guidance to our families. A spoken blessing is a positive, scriptural statement that invokes the blessing of God in the life of a child. The power of spoken blessings comes from God, Who Himself *"has blessed us with every spiritual blessing in the heavenly places in Christ"* (Ephesians 1:3). When we bless our children, we direct God's goodness to them; we intercede for them, we "stand in the gap" for them as we come boldly to the throne of grace in faith. There is a long history in the Bible of spoken blessings being passed down from generation to generation. When we pray for our children, God hears those prayers, as our words carry the weight and authority of heaven.

In Numbers 6:22-27, God instructs Moses and Aaron on just how to bless the people by pronouncing the following blessing over them: *"The Lord bless you, and keep you [protect you, sustain you, and guard you]; the Lord make His face shine upon you [with favour], and be gracious to you [surrounding you with lovingkindness]; the Lord lift up His countenance (face) upon you [with divine approval], and give you peace [a tranquil heart and life]. So Aaron and his sons shall put My name upon the children of Israel, and I will bless them." (AMP)*

23

Blessing your children marks them as God's own. In blessing your children, you are declaring words of truth over them. You are declaring words of scripture to be true about your child. You are verbally agreeing with Heaven about the truth over your child's identity and purpose. God told the patriarch Abraham: *"I will make you a great nation; I will bless you and make your name great; and you shall be a blessing. I will bless those who bless you, and I will curse him who curses you; and in you all the families of the earth shall be blessed"* (Gen. 12:2-3).

You can bless your children by speaking Abraham's blessing over them. Call your child, lay hands on them, and bless them by saying:
__(insert name)__, the Lord will make you a great nation; He will bless you and make your name great; and you shall be a blessing. The Lord will bless those who bless you, and He will curse him who curses you; and in you all the families of the earth shall be blessed. (Gen. 12:2-3)

Your children are a gift, a tremendous blessing from God. They are Israel's descendants, and they are to be known as the "seed of Abraham".

Words of Wisdom: The Bible frequently mentioned abundance as something God offers to those who trust in Him. A parent's obedience and faithfulness to God's Word can bring abundant blessings to their children.

Scripture Meditation: 2 Corinthians 9:8 (AMP)
"And God is able to make all grace [every favour and earthly

blessing] come in abundance to you, so that you may always [under all circumstances, regardless of the need] have complete sufficiency in everything [being completely self-sufficient in Him], and have an abundance for every good work and act of charity."

Your Declaration: I declare that the Lord has opened the floodgates of heaven over my children. Tremendous blessings are coming their way. They shall be satisfied with the goodness of God's house (Ps. 65:4). God's incredible blessings are over me and my family. We receive more than we have enough room to receive. The Lord brings us into a wealthy place. We are blessed with every spiritual blessing in heavenly places in Christ Jesus (Eph 1:3). My family walk in the double and triple harvest God has prepared for us. God continues to meet our needs according to the riches of His glory in Christ Jesus. The Lord will abundantly bless our provision (Ps 132:15). My family will be like a watered garden and like a spring of water whose waters do not fail (Isa. 58:11). My children will experience the surpassing greatness of God's favour. Men bless and favour my family every day because God daily loads us with benefits (Psalm 68:19). All nations will call my children blessed, for they will be a delightful land (Mal. 3:12). My family are blessed in our coming and blessed in our going out. Our vats overflow with abundance. Wherever my family go and whatever we do, we children are blessed. The earth shall yield her increase, and God shall bless my children. God shall bless my family with the abundance of heaven, and all the ends of the earth shall fear Him (Ps. 67:6-7). This is my prayer and declaration in Jesus' name.

PRAY FOR CHILDREN OF THE WORLD:

Pray that God should bless them like He blessed the seed of Abraham.

- WEEK 8 –

DECLARATIONS AGAINST DEBT & POVERTY

Living with debt in our consumer-driven society is considered normal, but God wants to break the spirit of debt and its bondage in our lives. The enemy uses debt as a tool to entrap people and keep them from God's purpose in their lives. It is an arrow he uses to bring shame and disgrace into a person's life. Your children will not be disgraced or put to shame in the name of Jesus. Inability to pay debt has led to a lot of people committing suicide. So many have lost their homes, and others have developed high blood pressure and other ailments because of debt.

Because of peer pressure, our children buy things they don't need with money they don't have, to impress people they don't know or even like! Lack of contentment has become a sickness in society. We buy to impress followers on social media to get likes and more followers. The more followers we have, the more pressure we get to impress! Living a fake life has become the norm.

When our children take on debt, they put themselves in bondage. The Bible instructs us to have no debt other than the debt of loving each other in the body of Christ. *"Owe nothing to anyone except to love and seek the best for one another; for he who [unselfishly] loves his neighbour has fulfilled the [essence of the] law [relating to one's fellowman]." (Romans 13:8 AMP)*. Apostle

Paul instructs us to learn to be satisfied in all things, whether in lack or abundance, through the power of our Lord Jesus Christ. *"But godliness with contentment is great gain. For we brought nothing into the world, and we can take nothing out of it." (1 Tim. 6:6-7).* True contentment comes from having faith that we will have everything we need in Christ. He is sufficient, and His promises are enough. I encourage us to learn to live within our budget and teach our children to do the same. Don't become enslaved through borrowing, as the borrower becomes a servant to the lender. I take hold of the anointing given to us by Christ and break the bondage of debt in your family. I proclaim the year of freedom (Jubilee) over your family in the name of Jesus!

Words of Wisdom: Greed and the love of money lead to a lack of contentment. You will not find contentment in things like people, possessions, or money, which hinder the pursuit of true happiness and satisfaction. I encourage you to pray for financial wisdom for your children and ask God to direct them onto the right path, so they don't become enslaved through borrowing, and when they are older, they will not depart from it. *"Train up a child in the way he should go [teaching him to seek God's wisdom and will for his abilities and talents], even when he is old he will not depart from it." (Prov. 22:6 - AMP)*

Scripture Meditation: 1 Timothy 6:6-12
"But godliness with contentment is great gain. For we brought nothing into the world, and we can take nothing out of it. But if we have food and clothing, we will be content with that. People who want to get rich fall into temptation and a trap and into many foolish and harmful desires that plunge men into ruin and

destruction. For the love of money is a root of all kinds of evil. Some people, eager for money, have wandered from the faith and pierced themselves with many griefs. But you, man of God, flee from all this, and pursue righteousness, godliness, faith, love, endurance and gentleness. Fight the good fight of the faith. Take hold of the eternal life to which you were called when you made your good confession in the presence of many witnesses."

Your Declaration: I declare that the spirit of debt will not ravage my children's lives. I loose my family from the curse of debt, poverty and lack in the name of Jesus. I command every mountain of debt to be removed and cast into the sea. Debt, hear the Word of the Lord and be removed from my children's lives in the name of Jesus! My children are debt-free. Every yoke of poverty is destroyed. The Holy Spirit leads them to make wise financial decisions. They are free from the curse of poverty and lack. God shall supply all my family's needs according to His riches in glory by Christ Jesus (Phil 4:19). The blessing of the Lord makes my family rich, and He adds no sorrow with it (Prov. 10:22). I break every curse of borrowing and loss and I command every financial mountain to be removed from my family in the name of Jesus. My children will not lack or go hungry. They lend unto many nations and borrow from none (Deut. 15:6). The destroyer will not destroy the prosperity of my family (Job 15:21). I bind and rebuke the spirit of debt. I destroy every altar of debt and poverty in my family. You spirit of debt assigned to hold my family bound, I command you to loose your hold in the mighty name of Jesus! I declare all debts cancelled in the name of Jesus. The yoke of financial debt is broken. God has created an opening of His abundant supernatural supply. He has opened the gates of heaven and poured out an abundance of blessings on my family. He has taken us from the land of loss to the land of increase and abundance of riches. We are free from the bondage and curse of debt, so we are no longer a slave to lenders. This is my prayer and declaration in Jesus' name.

PRAY FOR CHILDREN OF THE WORLD:

Pray that the Lord will take them from the land of loss to the land of increase and abundance.

- WEEK 9 -

DECLARATION OF BLESSINGS OVER JOB/CAREER

It is essential to ask for God's blessings over our jobs and careers. Anything we set out to do without God's blessing is meaningless. Ask the Lord to bless you and your family in the workplace. Commit all that you will do during the day into His hands. Before you leave home, sanctify the atmosphere of your workplace by pleading the blood of Jesus. Teach your children to do the same before they set out for the day. Ask the Lord to bless and establish the work of their hands and invite Jesus to be with you and your children throughout your workday.

"From the fruit of their lips people are filled with good things, and the work of their hands brings them reward." (Prov. 12:14 - NLT)

Whatever we do, whatever the task may be, we must put in our very best effort as something done for the Lord and not for men, knowing that it is from the Lord that we will receive our reward.

As you ask for God's blessing this week, also thank Him that everything will work out for your good and His glory. because He is with you and your children.

Words of Wisdom: When you ask for God's blessings over your jobs and career, He will use your talents and abilities for His glory and will bless the work of your hands. He will make you and your children exceedingly fruitful and prosperous. Teach your children to pray with another before they set out for the day. This also helps to build strong relationships with their siblings. This will bring your family closer to God, and closer to one another.

Scripture Meditation: Deut. 28: 12-13 (AMP)

"The Lord will open for you His good treasure house, the heavens, to give rain to your land in its season and to bless all the work of your hand; and you will lend to many nations, but you will not borrow. The Lord will make you the head (leader) and not the tail (follower); and you will be above only, and you will not be beneath, if you listen and pay attention to the commandments of the Lord your God, which I am commanding you today, to observe them carefully."

Your Declaration: I declare that the Lord gives my family great prosperity. We are blessed in our jobs and careers. Supernatural opportunities and breakthroughs will come our way. We will not be oppressed, harassed, or bullied by anyone at work. There is peace all around our work places. We will not be ashamed or disgraced. My children will not be afraid. They are victorious at work and abundantly blessed in all they lay their hands to do. They will not be stressed out. Thank you Lord for giving us colleagues at work who bless us every day with kind words and actions. We are content and happy in our jobs. God is lightening our burdens and taking the pressure off. We shall meet every one of our work targets in the name of Jesus. Our family will shine. The glory of God will be our rear guard (Isa. 58:8). Our jobs will not be touched by any economic downturn in the name of Jesus. We shall soar like eagles in our careers. We shall move forward in our jobs and careers. There is promotion and expansion. God will overwhelm my family with His goodness and amaze us with His favour. The Lord will do something in me and my children's career that the ears of everyone who hears it will tingle(1 Sam. 3:11). The Lord will bless all the work of our hands and we will testify of God's goodness and grace. This is my prayer and declaration in Jesus' name.

PRAY FOR CHILDREN OF THE WORLD:
That God will bless them with good jobs and careers and make the world a better place for all.

DECLARATIONS AGAINST UNEMPLOYMENT

From the fruit of their lips people are filled with good things, and the work of their hands brings them reward. (Prov. 12:14 - NIV)

Being unemployed is a difficult situation to be in. Many people are unable to find a job in the world in which we live, which is driving them to the brink of despair. God ordains work, and He uses our jobs to provide for necessities. The road to success requires a lot of effort and dedication, but it is not always an easy journey. A working Christian reflects an active God, Creator of the whole universe. We are not to be lazy because we represent a hardworking God. An idle life is a miserable, uncomfortable life. In 1 Timothy 5:8, the Bible states, *"But if anyone does not provide for his own, and especially for those of his household, he has denied the faith and is worse than an unbeliever."*

A hard worker has plenty of food, but a person who chases fantasies ends up in poverty (Prov. 28:19 - NLT)

Have you or your child not yet found employment? Continue searching. Continue to worship and thank God. Do not lose hope. The Lord will bring a job and open doors of opportunities to you. He will provide. Even in this period of unemployment, let your mouth continue to declare His praise. The Lord will calm your storm and ensure that no one in your family experiences poverty in the name of Jesus.

Words of Wisdom: *Whether you eat or drink or whatever you do, do it all for the glory of God. (1 Cor. 10:31).* Our children are to have nothing to do with idleness. Satan loves to find things for people to do. When we are not doing something productive with our time, this leads to more sin. If you or your child are unemployed and looking for a job, know that the Lord will provide. Keep God's peace in your heart.

Scripture Meditation: 2 Thessalonians 3:10-12
"For even while we were with you, we used to give you this order: if anyone is not willing to work, then he is not to eat, either. Indeed, we hear that some among you are leading an undisciplined and inappropriate life, doing no work at all, but acting like busybodies [meddling in other people's business]. Now such people we command and exhort in the Lord Jesus Christ to settle down and work quietly and earn their own food and other necessities [supporting themselves instead of depending on the hospitality of others]."

Your Declaration: I declare that the Lord has made crooked places straight and the rough places smooth before my family (Isa. 40:4). Every wall of unemployment and joblessness in my family is broken in the name of Jesus. Unemployment is of the past and will not be a problem ever again. The curse of idleness and poverty is broken. My family will not go begging for bread in the name of Jesus. When my children go for interviews, they will be favoured and not be worried, anxious or afraid. They will find the ideal position through the Lord's guidance. The Lord has broken off limitations and restrictions placed on my children's lives by any evil spirits. My family shall be satisfied with favour and full of the blessing of the Lord. The breaker is gone up before us and broken through every job limitation and barrier of the enemy (Mic. 2:13). The Lord gives my children the confidence to speak clearly and answer questions with wisdom at job interviews. He will lead them to the right job. In the name of Jesus, they will get phone calls, emails, and text messages with excellent news. Their blessing will not be swapped or stolen by the enemy. They flourish like a palm tree and grow like a cedar in Lebanon (Ps. 92:12). I declare that my family will be extremely prosperous (Gen. 30:43). We grow with the increase that is from God (Col. 2:19). The enemy will not be able to burn up our harvest. I rebuke, break and loose my children from all curses of unemployment in the name of Jesus. I rebuke the spirit of failure at the edge of their breakthrough. The curse of unemployment has been lifted from my family! This is my prayer and declaration in Jesus' name.

PRAY FOR CHILDREN OF THE WORLD:

That the curse of poverty and unemployment be broken in their lives.

DECLARATIONS
FOR DIVINE PROTECTION

In a world that is suffering threats of every type, including wars, rumours of war, disease, viral ailments, coronavirus outbreaks, delta, omicron, and all different kinds of variations, epidemics, and pandemics; it is reassuring to know that God has vowed to safeguard His people. He has made a shelter available for us to use. Psalm 61:3, *"For you have been a shelter for me, a strong tower from the enemy. I will abide in Your tabernacle forever; I will trust in the shelter of your wings."*

One day, when I was in prayer, the Lord reassured me that He has despatched His Angels to all corners of the earth to guard His children against the enemy's arrows, for the world is getting increasingly dark and deadly. These are dangerous times! He declared that wherever His children are on earth, His angels will guard and cover them. This guarantee applies to you and your family. Psalm 91:4 states, "He shall cover you with His feathers, and under His wings you shall take refuge." God Himself is our refuge and fortress, our secure haven. He is all-powerful and can always safeguard our home.

Other than physical security, there is nothing we can do to protect our children in school, college, university, the workplace, or anywhere else. We are limited as parents in our capability to defend ourselves, our children, or any other family member. We cannot do anything without Him. The enemy may set a trap, but we will not fall into it. The Lord has promised in Psalm 35 that the net they hid for us will catch themselves, and they will fall into their pit of destruction. *"For without cause they hid their net for me; without cause they dug a pit [of destruction] for my life. Let destruction come upon my enemy by surprise; let the net he hid for me catch him; into that very destruction let him fall. Then my soul shall rejoice in the LORD; it shall rejoice in His salvation"* (Ps. 35: 7-9 AMP). Thank you, Lord, for being our deliverer!

Words of Wisdom: Remember, since you have made the Lord your refuge and dwelling place, the danger will not approach you or your children. No misfortune will befall you, nor will any disease come near your home. The Lord is our protector. In Christ, you and your family are protected and secure. *"For He will command His angels in regard to you, to protect and defend and guard you in all your ways [of obedience and service]. They will lift you up in their hands, so that you do not [even] strike your foot against a stone."* (Ps. 91: 11-12 - AMP)

Scripture Meditation: Ps. 91: 7-8 – AMP
"A thousand may fall at your side and ten thousand at your right hand, but danger will not come near you. You will only [be a spectator as you] look on with your eyes and witness the [divine] repayment of the wicked [as you watch safely from the shelter of

the Most High]."

Your Declaration: I declare that the Lord is my family's hiding place. We dwell in the shelter of the Most High, and rest in the shadow of the Almighty. He is our refuge, our fortress, our God in whom we trust (Psalm 91:1-2). The Lord protects my family from trouble and surrounds us with songs of deliverance (Ps. 32:7). The Lord preserves us from all evil. He preserves our souls. He preserves our going out and coming in from this time and forevermore (Ps. 121:7-8). My children walk securely because they walk in integrity (Prov. 10:9). They shall not be afraid of the terror by night, the arrow that flies by day, the pestilence that walks in darkness, or the destruction that lays waste at noonday (Ps. 91: 5-6). The Lord keeps my family in His loving care. He keeps us as the apple of His eye and hides us in the protective shadow of His wings. He is our refuge and strength, mighty and impenetrable, an ever-present help in trouble (Ps. 46:1). He will cover my children with His feathers, and they will find refuge under His wings. God's truth will be my family's shield and buckler (Ps. 91:4). The sun shall not smite us by day nor the moon by night (Ps.121:6). The Lord is faithful; He will strengthen and protect my children from the evil one (2 Thess. 3:3). When sicknesses or any terrible diseases see the blood of Jesus on me and my children, they must pass over (Exod. 12:13). No harm will overtake us in the name of Jesus. I plead the blood of Jesus on every member of my family and my home. The Lord will set my family securely on high because we know His name; we confidently trust and rely on Him, knowing He will never abandon us, no, never. This is my prayer and declaration in Jesus' name.

> **PRAY FOR CHILDREN OF THE WORLD:**
>
> That the Lord will be their ever-present help in trouble.
>
> He will protect and keep them from the evil one.

DECLARATIONS
OF VICTORY

Are you praying for God to give you the strength and courage you need to get through the storm of ongoing trials and tribulations in your family? In Mark 4:38, the disciples were thrown around in an unexpected storm, prompting them to ask Jesus, "Master, do you not care that we are perishing?" They were navigating turbulent waters and prayed for relief by asking for help. You may be experiencing a comparable storm in your family and asking Jesus, "...do you not care that we are perishing?" I'm sure you can relate to the disciples when you're thrown around in life's unforeseen storms, pleading with the Lord not to "sleep through" whatever crisis you're facing.

The disciples felt Jesus was uninterested in them, that He didn't care about them or the storms they were going through, but He revealed that he cares about them more than anyone else, and He delivered them from their despair. In Jesus, there is no lack of concern or affection. He genuinely cares about you and your children. You may be unable to see what Jesus is doing in your circumstance, but I want you to know that He is working to calm the storm of worry, fear, despair, and hopelessness that you and your children are experiencing. He invites you to put your faith in His love and cling to His peace that surpasses all understanding. If Jesus is on board, your family will never experience a shipwreck. He will quiet any storm and restore peace to your situation. When you have Jesus on board, the wreckage of your children's future will not occur because God will be your source of strength. He will turn bad outcomes into good ones. The Lord will continue to show up for you and your family and bring you victory. He creates a path where there is none. Don't worry; Jesus will not "sleep through" your crises. Your story will undoubtedly end in praise to Him!

Words of Wisdom: If you are going through a time when it seems God is nowhere to be found. He will arise in your storm. When the disciples called on Jesus, *"He arose, rebuked the wind, and said to the sea, "Peace, be still!" And the wind ceased and there was great calm" (Mark4:39).* Call on Him and be confident that Jesus will arise for you too. He will arise on behalf of your children. He will arise amid your storm, and there will be great calm for you. I rebuke every storm in your family in the name of Jesus! Be anxious for nothing. Don't be afraid, have faith. Jesus has risen!

Scripture Meditation: Deuteronomy 20:3-4 (AMP)
"...Do not lack courage. Do not be afraid, or panic, or tremble [in terror] before them, for the LORD your God is He who goes with you, to fight for you against your enemies, to save you."

Your Declaration: I declare thanksgiving unto God who gives me and my children victory through our Lord Jesus Christ (1 Cor. 15:57). We experience great victories, supernatural turnarounds, and miraculous breakthroughs in the midst of great impossibilities. The sceptre of evil and wickedness will not rest on my family in the name of Jesus (Ps. 125:3). No matter what happens and whatever we go through, we are more than conquerors through Him who loved us (Rom. 8:37). In all things, I declare we gain an overwhelming victory through Him who loved us. I declare victory in every situation, we win and shall lose no battle in the name of Jesus. I declare thanksgiving unto God who leads us in triumph in Christ, and through us diffuses the fragrance of His knowledge in every place (2 Cor. 2:14). Our hearts will not faint, we will not be scared, we will not quiver or be terrified because of the adversary, because the Lord our God is with us, fighting for my family against our foes and saving us. He has brought our enemies down by His hands in the name of Jesus. The victory of the Word is our victory in the name of Jesus. The kingdom of darkness has no power over us. My family are of God, and have overcome Satan, because He who is in us is greater than he who is in the world" (1 John 4:4). We are victorious by the blood of Jesus! This is my prayer and declaration in Jesus' name.

PRAY FOR CHILDREN OF THE WORLD:
That the Lord will go with them to fight against their enemies, to save them.

- WEEK 13 –

DECLARATIONS
FOR BREAKTHROUGHS

Are you praying for a breakthrough for your child? Are there serious situations at home you are praying for God to intervene? Let me encourage and reassure you that God is a God of breakthrough! You can rely on His character. God's character, His nature and His heart never change. I want you to have confidence and faith in Him that He is the God of your breakthrough! God's ways are higher than ours. As parents, the battle we face every day is to trust His heart even in the face of insurmountable odds in the family and believe in God for the impossible. You can trust Him to provide your breakthrough in your time of need. If you feel like you are constantly in survival mode with your children because everywhere you turn, one of them needs a breakthrough, and it's one battle after the other. Do not give up; your breakthrough is near.

Do you recall the biblical narrative of Joseph? He progressed from a state of breakdown to one of breakthrough. The same God of breakthrough is now communicating with you. He is forever faithful!

In the Book of John, Jesus said, *"I have told you these things, so that in Me you may have [perfect] peace. In the world, you have tribulation and distress and suffering, but be courageous [be confident, be undaunted, be filled with joy]; I have overcome the* world." [My conquest is accomplished, My victory abiding.]" (John 16:33 AMP). It is easy to get discouraged when the mountains seem insurmountable but remember that God's promise has already conquered the earth through His Son, Jesus! Breakthrough is not just what God does; it is who He is. The Lord will break through your enemies before you, like a breakthrough of water in the name of Jesus. (2 Sam. 5:20)

Words of Wisdom: Pray for the precise breakthroughs your family require from God and write down what you want to see as an outcome of your breakthrough, which will become your testimony. Then, pray God's Word back to Him. The importance of praying the Bible aloud for spiritual breakthroughs cannot be overstated. It pierces the enemy's defences and shatters them! God's spoken word is far more potent than we can imagine. As a result, our wants and perceptions are aligned with His, resulting in spiritual breakthroughs. Thank the Lord for the answer.

For example, you could write as a title, "God of my Breakthrough", and then, in the following few lines, write:

1) "I thank you, Lord, for breaking through in (_____)'s life."
2) "I thank you for breaking through in (_____)'s education and exams."
3) "I thank you for breaking through in (_____)'s mental health and healing him/her."

You can build your own list of things to be thankful for in your family by drawing inspiration from the examples shared above.

Scripture Meditation: 2 Samuel 5:19-20 (AMP)

"David inquired of the Lord, saying, "Shall I go up against the Philistines? Will You hand them over to me?" And the Lord said to David, "Go up, for I will certainly hand them over to you." So, David came to Baal-perazim, and he defeated them there, and said, "The Lord has broken through my enemies before me, like a breakthrough of water." So, he named that place Baal-perazim (master of breakthroughs)."

Your Declaration: I declare breakthroughs are coming into my family. My children will not continually struggle. The Lord is the God of our breakthroughs. We have broken forth against our enemies like a breakthrough of water (2 Sam 5:20). Every barrier is broken, and hindrances are removed in the name of Jesus. My children's days of difficulties are over; they have broken through. I dismantle every opposition fighting against their breakthroughs in the name of Jesus. God is ushering in new seasons of growth in my family. We have a strong family and a strong city (Isa. 26:1). There is an anointing of ease in my children's lives. God has anointed my family with the oil of gladness more than our companions (Ps. 45:7). We are successful. My children rise above every difficulty and will not let people or circumstances upset them. I demolish every satanic wall of Jericho built around my family. (Josh. 6:5). God has gone before us, making crooked places straight. The Lord will establish peace for us (Isa. 26:12). We will be glad and rejoice in His salvation (Isa.25:9). This is my prayer and declaration in Jesus' name.

PRAY FOR CHILDREN OF THE WORLD:

Pray that every barrier is broken, and hindrances removed.

- WEEK 14 –

DECLARATIONS AGAINST THE ENEMY

We all know that the devil and his followers are our family's biggest enemy. He is always looking for ways to attack the children of God through all of his different ways and plans. When we obey God and trust Him, we will win in the name of Jesus. We are aware that the enemy covets our children and that he intends to snatch them from us to further his agenda. According to the Bible, he prowls around like a roaring lion looking for someone to devour. Therefore, parents, it is highly advised that we always "Be sober" (meaning "well balanced and self-disciplined"), as well as "Be alert and cautious." *"That adversary of yours, the devil, roams the earth like a roaring lion that is ravenously hungry, looking for someone to devour"* (1 Peter 5:8). We also know that Satan is cunning and tries to lure our children away from us in many ways, including tempting them, distracting them, tricking them, etc. But the book of 1 Peter chapter 5 verse 9 encourages us to *"... Resist him, and be firm in your faith [against his attack—rooted, established, and immovable]..."*

When we pray to God, asking for the protection of our children from the dangers of the world, we should remember that we are not praying to a far-off God who is inaccessible to us in any way. No! We are praying to the King who reigns over all kings and Lord who reigns over all lords! His name is Emmanuel, which means "God with us." He is also known as the great I AM, and He is the one who loves and treasures the souls of our children more than we could ever think or imagine.

We thank God for making us more than conquerors in Christ. *"But thanks be to God, who gives us the victory [as conquerors] through our Lord Jesus Christ,"* writes I Corinthians 15:57. *"Yet in all these things we are more than conquerors, having won an unfathomable victory through Him who loved us [so much that He died for us]"* (Rom. 8:37).

Words of Wisdom: In 2 Chronicles 20, when Jehoshaphat, the king of Judah, received word that three of his enemies were plotting an attack on him and the people of God. What exactly did he do to ensure his success? First, he singled out the adversary, refusing to turn a blind eye to the issue. Second, he resolved to find the Lord and publicly declared that he would fast during this time. Have you been praying and fasting about your situation? The power of prayer is essential to winning. Thirdly, Jehoshaphat did not rely solely on himself to achieve victory. At this very moment, you must converse with God and ask for His assistance, as you cannot prevail against the adversary alone. You need the divine intervention of the Lord. *"My grace is sufficient for you [My lovingkindness and My mercy are more than enough—always available—regardless of the situation]; for [My] power is being perfected [and is completed and shows itself most effectively] in [your] weakness." (2 Corinthians 12:9) AMP*

God's grace is sufficient for you and your children. His lovingkindness and mercy are more than enough, always available regardless of the situation.

Scripture Meditation: Psalm 3:6-8

"I will not be intimidated or afraid of the ten thousands who have set themselves against me all around. Arise, O Lord; save me, O my God! For You have struck all my enemies on the cheek; You have shattered the teeth of the wicked. Salvation belongs to the Lord; May Your blessing be upon Your people."

Your Declaration: I declare that the enemy will not be able to outwit my children, nor will the son of wickedness afflict my family. The Lord will destroy our adversaries in front of our eyes and bring calamity upon those who hate us (Ps. 89:22-23). When the enemy comes in like a flood, the Spirit of the Lord will raise a standard against him (Isa. 59:19). I call upon the holy warrior Angels of God to protect and shield my family from demonic attacks. None of the enemy's evil schemes will succeed over my children in the name of Jesus. By the power in the name of Jesus we push down our enemies, in His name we trample our foes (Ps. 44:5). The Lord gives us victory over our enemies and disgraces those who hate us (Ps. 44:7). Because of God, my family can outrun an army. By Him, we can leap over a wall (Ps. 18:29). The Lord gives my children the ability to overcome any obstacle and makes their path flawless. They can stand firmly and walk confidently along paths of testing and trouble because the Lord establishes them securely upon their high places. My family are supported and held up by the right hand of God and will not fall. We do not suffer loss in conflict; instead, we emerge victoriously. The enemy has fallen under our feet in the name of Jesus (Ps. 18:38). My children are great because the Lord has brought them out into a broad place, held them up with His right hand, and made them great with his gentleness. It is God who takes vengeance for my children and who brings their adversaries to submission under them. He saves my family from the hands of the enemy and exalts us above those who have taken up arms against us. Great deliverance He gives to my family and shows us His mercy. This is my prayer and declaration in Jesus' name.

PRAY FOR CHILDREN OF THE WORLD:
That the Lord will light their lamp and enlighten their darkness.

- WEEK 15 –

DECLARATIONS
OF WARFARE PRAYERS

We cannot afford to be indifferent when it comes to spiritual battles. The forces of evil are waging a spiritual war for our children's hearts, attempting to pull them away from God and alienate them from Him. We must be mindful of the strategies of the devil. Until Jesus arrives, we are engaged in daily warfare. I encourage all parents to participate in the supernatural battle against the powers of evil and to stand in God's authority for their family by the power in the name of Jesus. The enemy is a strategist and a tactician. He has come to steal, kill, and destroy. He is out to destroy families who identify with Christ. As a result, we must pursue the enemy and prevent him from plotting against our children. Satan is vehemently and purposefully opposed to God's work in your family and home. His plans must be destroyed by the power of prayer in the name of Jesus.

In Ephesians 6:10-13 *(NLT)*, Apostle Paul encourages us to put on the whole armour of God. *"A final word: Be strong in the Lord and in his mighty power. Put on all of God's armour so that you will be able to stand firm against all strategies of the devil. For we are not fighting against flesh-and-blood enemies, but against evil rulers and authorities of the unseen world, against mighty powers in this dark world, and against evil' spirits in the heavenly places. Therefore, put on every piece of God's armour so you will be able to resist the enemy in the time of evil. Then after the battle you will still be standing firm.*

Dear parents, God warns us that the threat of spiritual warfare is extremely real and must be taken seriously and that we should prepare ourselves with the resources He has provided us with to combat it. Our most challenging battle in life is not with what we can see but with what we can't see. The Bible states that "We do not wrestle against flesh and blood, but against principalities, against powers, against the rulers of the darkness of this age, against spiritual hosts of wickedness in the heavenly places." Therefore, we must take up the whole armour of God and wage battle for the lives of our children and families at all times.

Words of Wisdom: With these lines in Ephesians 6:18, Paul encourages us to "pray at all times in the Spirit, which is the Word of God, praying always with all prayer and supplication in the Spirit" and to "make supplication for the saints," he is referring to the church's prayer life. His point of view is that we should constantly pray and be in a state of readiness for combat. Therefore, our lives must include significant time spent in warfare prayers.

Scripture Meditation: 2 Corinthians 10:3-5 (AMP)
"For though we walk in the flesh [as mortal men], we are not carrying on our [spiritual] warfare according to the flesh and using the weapons of man. The weapons of our warfare are not physical [weapons of flesh and blood]. Our weapons are divinely powerful for the destruction of fortresses. We are destroying sophisticated arguments and every exalted and proud thing that sets itself up against the [true] knowledge of God, and we are taking every

thought and purpose captive to the obedience of Christ"

Your Declaration: I declare that the Lord hides my family from the secret plots of the wicked and from the rebellion of the workers of iniquity (Ps. 64:2). He will make our enemies stumble over their own tongues (Ps. 64:8). The sword of the wicked assigned against my family shall enter their own hearts. Their bows shall break in the name of Jesus! (Ps. 37:15). We are delivered from the power of the lions (Dan. 6:27). The sun shall not strike my children by day nor the moon by night (Ps. 121:6). The foot of pride will not come against my family. The hand of the wicked will not drive us away (Ps. 36:11). The Lord will not allow my children's foot to be moved (Ps. 121:3). When the enemy comes in like a flood, the Spirit of the LORD will lift a standard against him (Isa. 59:19). The sons of those who afflict my family shall come bowing to us. All those who despised us shall fall prostrate at the soles of our feet. They shall call us "The City of the Lord, Zion of the Holy One of Israel" (Isa. 60:14). The Lord will repay our enemies according to their deeds. He will repay fury to our adversaries and recompense to our enemies (Isa.59:18). I command you, devils, to leave my family right now in the name of Jesus! (Mark 7:29). Evil will not visit our home (Prov.19:23). I rebuke all enemies and agents that Satan has assigned to attack my children and our entire family in the name of Jesus. The Lord will be a wall of fire protecting us from enemies, and He will be the glory in our midst (Zech. 2:5). I plead the blood of Jesus against all the plans of evil and bind the attacking forces of Satan in the name of Jesus. I command all the powers of darkness assigned against my family to bow down to the Lordship of Jesus Christ. This is my prayer and declaration in Jesus' name.

> ## PRAY FOR CHILDREN OF THE WORLD:
> That the Lord will transform their lives and be a wall of fire around them.

DECLARATIONS
FOR DELIVERANCE

I have good news for you: God is our Deliverer! The biblical story of Shadrach, Meshach, and Abednego being miraculously saved from the burning fiery furnace by God is an example of the fact that only God can deliver people from danger. His deliverance is far greater than anything our sorrows could be.

In Daniel chapter 3, these three men, who were servants of the Lord, were cast into a blazing furnace because they disobeyed the king's order to worship a golden image. *"Whoever does not fall down and worship will immediately be thrown into a blazing furnace."* Nebuchadnezzar had enacted a decree. *"Shadrach, Meshach, and Abed-Nego answered and said to the king, "O Nebuchadnezzar, we do not need to answer you in this matter. If that is the case, our God whom we serve is able to deliver us from the burning fiery furnace, and He will deliver us from your hand, O king. But if not, let it be known to you, O king, that we do not serve your gods, nor will we worship the gold image which you have set up." (Daniel 3:16-18)*

When Shadrach, Meshach, and Abednego were ultimately cast into the burning furnace, they survived unscathed because the God they had trusted sent His Angel to guard them. The fire had no power, the hair on their head was not singed nor were their garments affected, and the smell of fire was not on them (Daniel

3:27). It's nothing less than a miracle! The great Deliverer is our God!

Can you see a miracle happening in your family as well? You are not alone; you have a Deliverer. The Bible states in Psalm 34:19, *Many are the afflictions of the righteous, but the Lord delivers him out of them all."* The Lord will turn your mourning into dancing, and He will lift your burdens from your shoulders in the name of Jesus.

Words of Wisdom: The Christian life is not without hardships, troubles, and challenges. Families encounter afflictions on a regular basis. However, I encourage you to recognise God as your family's ultimate Deliverer. You will see Him deliver your family from the blazing furnace and the roaring demons of life if you put your confidence in Him. God's help is on its way to you. God will turn the difficulties you are going through into opportunities for the advancement of the Kingdom. Please bear in mind that God's deliverance is going to be much bigger than the problems you face!

Scripture Meditation: Psalm 18:2-3
"The Lord is my rock and my fortress and my deliverer; my God, my strength, in whom I will trust; my shield and the horn of my salvation, my stronghold. I will call upon the Lord, who is worthy to be praised; so shall I be saved from my enemies."

Your Declaration: I declare that my family are free from evil demonic witchcraft attacks, sickness, pain, dream attacks, conflicts, fear, oppression, depression, and the enemy's arrows.

We are no longer subjected to demonic assaults on our lives and possessions. You, LORD, are a shield around my family, our glory, and the One who lifts our heads high (Ps. 3:3). I cry out to the LORD on behalf of my children and family, and He answers me from His holy mountain. My family sleeps and wakes up because the LORD takes care of us and keeps us safe. The Lord is our rock and strength in whom we put our faith, our shield and horn of deliverance, our high tower and fortress (Ps. 18:2). My children are delivered by the hand of God from the lion's mouth. The Lord delivers them from evil and draws them closer to Himself. They are set free from every evil work and protected for God's glorious Kingdom (2 Tim. 4:18). The Lord preserves my children from trouble. He surrounds them with songs of deliverance (Ps. 32:7). Surely, the Lord will deliver my children from the fowler's trap and the deadly pestilence. He will protect them under His wings and cover them with His feathers. His faithfulness will be my family's shield and defence. We will not be terrified of the terrors of the night, the arrow that flies during the day, the pestilence that stalks in the dark, or the plague that destroys at midday. A thousand may fall at our side, ten thousand at our right hand, but danger will not come near any one of my children or family. We will only look with our eyes and see the reward of the wicked in the name of Jesus (Ps. 91:7-8). Because we acknowledge His Name, the Lord will rescue and protect us. We will call on the Lord's name, and He will answer; He will be with my family in trouble, delivering and honouring us. With long and healthy life, He will satisfy my family and show us His salvation. This is my prayer and declaration in Jesus' name.

PRAY FOR CHILDREN OF THE WORLD:

That the Lord will be their refuge, shelter, and deliverer.

- WEEK 17 –

DECLARATIONS
FOR EXAM SUCCESS

From primary to secondary school, College to University and beyond, our children's lives are full of times challenging and demanding them to be at their best. Being a Christian in school can be difficult, plus the added pressure of exams. The week before exams and finals are two of the most challenging weeks a student will experience. There are fears, tears, anxiety, books flung here and there, lots of junk food and sleeplessness. Your children soon learn that education requires hard work and more of their time and resources. But you don't have to worry; no exam is higher than God's power. Your children may feel tired and weak during finals week, yet we have an amazing God who will renew their strength and make it all worth it.

Keep praying and thanking God for renewing their strength so they will not give up during this difficult time. He alone can make them excel and succeed in their exams, as there is nothing too difficult for Him. *"Even the youths shall faint and be weary, and the young men shall utterly fall, but those who wait on the Lord shall renew their strength; they shall mount up with wings like eagles, they shall run and not be weary, they shall walk and not faint (Isaiah 40:29-31)."*

We have an awesome God who assures us that everything will be okay. God is entirely in control of your children's exams, destiny, and results. Do not worry about what is outside your control. God will help your children in their time of need. The God you believe in is bigger than anything you or your children may face. *"But Jesus looked at them and said to them, "With men this is impossible, but with God all things are possible (Matt. 19: 26)."* Keep trusting Him. He will never fail you.

Words of Wisdom: The Lord is with your children. He will go before them, and He will not leave them nor forsake them. He plans to give your children a future and hope. *"Be strong and of good courage, do not fear nor be afraid of them; for the Lord your God, He is the One who goes with you. He will not leave you nor forsake you (Deut. 31:6)."* Use the scriptures to pray for them. He will show Himself strong on your children's behalf. *"For the eyes of the Lord run to and fro throughout the whole earth, to show Himself strong on behalf of those whose heart is loyal to Him (2 Chron. 16:9)."* Use the scriptures to pray for them. He will show Himself strong on your children's behalf. *"For the eyes of the Lord run to and fro throughout the whole earth, to show Himself strong on behalf of those whose heart is loyal to Him (2 Chron. 16:9)."*

Scripture Meditation: Philippians 4: 6-7
"Do not be anxious or worried about anything, but in everything [every circumstance and situation] by prayer and petition with thanksgiving, continue to make your [specific] requests known to God. And the peace of God [that peace which reassures the heart, that peace] which transcends all understanding, [that peace which] stands guard over your hearts and your minds in Christ Jesus [is yours]."

Your Declaration: I declare that the spirit of diligence is upon my children as they approach the period of exams. God increases their ability to study. As they study for their exams, soak up knowledge and memorise facts, God renews their minds and strengthens their spirit. The Lord blankets them in His peace as they enter the exam hall. He helps them focus on the task at hand. He eases any anxieties and calms their restless mind. God is entirely in control of their exams, destiny, and results. They will be able to prepare well for the exams. They have the spirit of excellence within them and will do exceptionally well in all of their exams. They will answer each question with ease, confidence and peace of mind. God grants them favour in the eyes of the examiners (Daniel 1:9). When examiners see their papers, they will have no choice but to give them excellent marks. They will succeed and do well, giving God all the glory. The Holy Spirit will lead and guide their focus on relevant areas to the questions in their forthcoming exams. My children retain all information pertaining to their exams. They have knowledge and understanding (Daniel 1:17). They are not anxious or worried during their exams. I cast out every fear and doubt in the name of Jesus. My children trust the Lord with all their heart and do not lean on their own understanding. During their exams, they acknowledge the Lord, and He shall direct their paths (Prov. 3:5-6). They can do all things through Christ who strengthens them (Phil. 4:13). They soar on wings like eagles (Isa. 40:31). Their confidence is in God and not in their own ability. God renews their energy levels (Isa. 40:31). They will succeed and not fail because Christ dwells richly in them. I declare success in their exams in the name of Jesus. Failure is not their portion. They will not give up. This is my prayer and declaration in Jesus' name.

PRAY FOR CHILDREN OF THE WORLD:

Pray God increases their ability to study; they succeed in life and not fail.

- WEEK 18 –

DECLARATIONS AGAINST SICKNESS & INFIRMITY

There was no sickness, pain, or death before the fall of man, but we live in a fallen, wicked world, and the reality of human frailty is too present for us to ignore – if we continue in ignorance, it will harm us further. In the Book of 1 Kings 17:20-22, God miraculously provided for Elijah at the widow's home who lived in Zarephath, but the joy was short-lived because her son became sick. Her son's illness was so severe that no breath was left in him, and he died. The widow of Zarephath lamented by accusing Elijah of bringing sorrow to her home, so Elijah took the boy from his mother into the upper room. *"Then he cried out, "O Lord my God, have You brought further tragedy to the widow I am staying with by causing her son to die? Then he stretched himself out on the boy three times and cried to the LORD, "O Lord my God, please let this child's life return to him. The LORD heard Elijah's cry, and the boy's life returned to him, and he lived."*

This story shows God's power over sickness and the worst part of sickness - death. Let us remember that our God is the God of impossibilities, the One who has inexhaustible power, who never has and will never meet a threatening obstacle He cannot overcome or an aggressive enemy He cannot defeat. Because of Elijah's faith in the God of impossibilities, not even death caused him to doubt. God's desire for us is to be healed, and there is no sickness or disease outside of His control. Healing is the will of

God. He is a good, good Father and worthy of our trust. Jesus died and rose for our sins, sicknesses and diseases. The Bible states in Isaiah 53:5, *"He was wounded for our transgressions and crushed for our wickedness [our sin, injustice and wrongdoing]; the punishment for our well-being fell on Him, and by His stripes (wounds) we are healed."*

Our Lord is moved with compassion for what you and your family face today. Jesus says, "I am willing to make you and your children whole." He is our healer, helper, and compassionate friend.

Words of Wisdom: Jesus feels compassion and sympathy for you and your family. He is saying, "I am willing to do whatever it takes to help you and your children." He is your healer, helper, and compassionate friend.

Scripture Meditation: Mark 1:40-42

"And a leper came to Him, begging Him and falling on his knees before Him, saying, "If You are willing, You are able to make me clean." Moved with compassion [for his suffering], Jesus reached out with His hand and touched him, and said to him, "I am willing; be cleansed." The leprosy left him immediately and he was cleansed [completely healed and restored to health]."

Your Declaration: I declare that the Lord protects my children from all sickness (Deut. 7:15). Their immune system grows stronger daily. The Word of God flows to every cell and organ in their body, restoring and transforming their health. Jesus Christ bore their sicknesses and carried their pain. Therefore there is no place for illness or pain in their body. Sickness is illegal and has no right to cling to me or my children. Tumours or growths will not live in our bodies. Our body is the temple of the Holy Spirit, and every organ in our body functions the way God intended. The Lord will fulfil the number of our days (Ex. 23:26). He will satisfy my family with long life and show us His salvation (Ps. 91:16). I break every stronghold over my children's lives in the name of Jesus! No evil disease will cleave to their body(Ps. 41:8). I break the power of illness and rebuke all curses of sickness and infirmity in my family in the name of Jesus. My children are free from infection and disease by the power in the name of Jesus. They are healed and set free from every curse of sickness in the name of Jesus. They walk in divine health, and no sickness or plague will come near their dwelling (Ps. 91:10). My family shall live and not die (Ps. 118:17). We are redeemed from sickness and disease (Gal. 3:13). This is my prayer and declaration in Jesus' name.

PRAY FOR CHILDREN OF THE WORLD:

Pray that the Lord will fulfil the number of their days and satisfy them with long life.

- WEEK 19 –

DECLARATIONS AGAINST MENTAL ATTACKS

If your child is feeling depressed and anxious or weary and worried, please know that God wants to meet them through the power of prayer. Seeing a child suffering or going through mental health challenges is hugely distressing for any parent. Understandably, as parents, we want to "fix" anything that causes our children pain. However, it is an actual reality that anybody can struggle with their mental health, whether the person is young or old, a believer or unbeliever. Mental illness is a part of living in a fallen world. If your son/daughter suffers from mental health challenges, I want you to know you are not alone. Our prayers are with you. God is with you, no matter where you find yourself today or any day in the future. Be determined not to give up on that child (your gift from God).

Because of God's plan and purpose, the enemy is fighting over your children's destinies. The Bible encourages us to "Set your mind on things above, not on things on earth." (Col. 3:2). God can turn your pain, sadness, and mourning into dancing again. "You have turned my mourning into dancing for me; you have taken off my sackcloth and clothed me with joy" (Psalm 30:11).

God formed your children's inward parts. He knit them together in your womb. As a result, they are beautiful, fearfully and wonderfully made (Ps. 139:14). Reciting, memorising, and meditating on Bible verses can help your children feel better and realign their thoughts to God, which will help them better fight off anxiety, negative self-image, or depression.

Words of Wisdom: Praying with your child unto God about their struggles will benefit and strengthen them. Understand that God can help your children live a life of servitude to Him. Don't give up on that troubled child. God has not given up on them. He will never forsake you or your children. Continue decreeing, confessing the Word, and pleading the blood of Jesus over your children's minds and thoughts, and Jesus will help you overcome. Your family's story will end in praise in the mighty name of Jesus.

Scripture Meditation: Philippians 4:8 (AMP)
"Finally, believers, whatever is true, whatever is honourable and worthy of respect, whatever is right and confirmed by God's word, whatever is pure and wholesome, whatever is lovely and brings peace, whatever is admirable and of good repute; if there is any excellence, if there is anything worthy of praise, think continually on these things [center your mind on them, and implant them in your heart]."

Your Declaration: I declare that no weapon of mental attacks formed against my family shall prosper in the name of Jesus. I rebuke and condemn every tongue that rises against my family in judgment (Isa. 54:17). I break free and loose my children from all psychic heredity, demonic strongholds and bondage of physical and mental illnesses resulting from generational sins. My children are free from the spirits of madness and confusion that would attempt to oppress their minds. I bind the spirit of instability and double mindedness over my family in the name of Jesus (James 1:8). My children are free from oppression. I break all generational curses of insanity, bipolar, schizophrenia, unworthiness, discouragement, suicide, rage, alcoholism, and hopelessness in the name of Jesus. My children are established in righteousness and they are far from oppression. Terror shall not come near my home (Isa. 54:14). My children are a beautiful work of God. They are fearfully and wonderfully created in the image and likeness of God (Ps 139:14). They are valuable and will value themselves. They will prosper and be in health even as their soul prospers (3 John 2). By the stripes of Jesus, my children are healed and delivered from plagues and evil spirits (Luke 7:21). Neither death, nor life, nor angels, nor rulers, nor things present, nor things to come, nor powers, nor height, nor depth, nor anything else in all creation, will be able to separate my family from the love of God in Christ Jesus our Lord (Romans 8:38-39). This is my prayer and declaration in Jesus' name.

PRAY FOR CHILDREN OF THE WORLD:

That God sets them free from spirits of madness and confusion.

- WEEK 20

DECLARATIONS AGAINST FEAR & ANXIETY

In the Book of Job 5:7, the Bible states that man is born for trouble. The harsh reality of the human experience is that we will all face challenges during our lives. It is easy to advise other people in their trouble, but a day will come when we must now obey our own advice, which reminds me of the story of Jehoshaphat in 2 Chronicles 20, where the king needed to take his own advice. Chapter 19:11 ends with Jehoshaphat's words when he spoke to the people and encouraged them. He said, "Behave courageously, and the LORD will be with the good."

Things were going very well for this good king who was loyal and obedient to God. Then there was sudden trouble! Two countries that were the king's neighbours sent their armies with help from some other nations and came to attack Judah, where Jehoshaphat ruled. Now Jehoshaphat had a significant problem with anxiety and fear. The king needed to take his own advice. It was natural for him to be very anxious and afraid, as he had no military strength. He only had a small army and was not prepared. God was their only chance to help. He knew his people could never overcome the enemy and needed his own advice now his worst fears were happening. He was so anxious and afraid!

What did Jehoshaphat do when he was anxious?
He set himself to **seek** the Lord (vs 3)

He proclaimed a **fast** throughout all Judah (vs 3)

They gathered together to **ask help** from the Lord (vs 4)

He **remembers God's goodness** in the former days (vs 6-10)

Words of Wisdom: Because Jehoshaphat was anxious, he hurried to the place of prayer. Don't be worried or afraid when things go wrong in the family. When in trouble, do not let anxiety or fear control your thoughts. Good things can result from our problems. Remember God's love towards you and your children in the past. Think about how good He has been to you. The God who was with you then will not forget you now. In your trouble, do not forget that God rules. When you are anxious about family issues, like Jehoshaphat, hurry to the place of prayer!

Scripture Meditation: 2 Chronicles 20:17

You will not need to fight in this battle. Position yourselves, stand still and see the salvation of the Lord, who is with you, O Judah and Jerusalem!' Do not fear or be dismayed; tomorrow go out against them, for the Lord is with you."

Your Declaration: I declare that no one shall make my family afraid, for the mouth of the LORD of hosts has spoken (Micah 4:4). When anxiety is great within my family, God's consolation brings us peace. We will not be afraid of ten thousands of people who have set themselves against us all around (Ps. 3:6). No matter what happens, my children will live unafraid. They will not be afraid or dismayed, for the Lord is with them (2 Chron. 20:17). They are taught of the Lord, and great is their peace (Isa. 54:13). They do not have the spirit of fear but power, love, and a sound mind (2 Tim. 1:7). God's perfect peace calms my children in every circumstance and gives them courage and strength for every challenge. They will not be afraid of the arrow that flies by day or the terror that comes at night (Ps. 91:5). I bind and rebuke any spirit that would creep against my family at night. I rebuke bad dreams and nightmares in the name of Jesus. We will rest at night because the Lord gives us peace. We will not be anxious about anything, but in every situation, by prayer and petition, we present our requests to God with thanksgiving, and the peace of God, which surpasses all understanding, will guard our hearts and minds through Christ Jesus (Phil. 4: 6-7). My children will dwell in safety; nothing and no one shall make my family anxious or afraid (Ezek. 34:28). I banish anxiety and stress from my family and command all hereditary spirits of fear and anxiety to come out of our lives in the mighty name of Jesus! This is my prayer and declaration in Jesus' name.

PRAY FOR CHILDREN OF THE WORLD:

That God will deliver them from anxiety and fear.

DECLARATIONS
FOR EMOTIONAL HEALING

"The righteous cry out, and the Lord hears them; he delivers them from all their troubles. The Lord is close to the broken-hearted and saves those who are crushed in spirit." Psalm 34:17-18 (NIV)

Being heartbroken and hurt is a sad reality for most of us. At some point in our lives, we all need emotional healing to one degree or another. While growing up, we have all experienced different kinds of hurt. Whether the cause is natural or because of another's sin, most of us fight some emotional battle. Due to our society today, it is very challenging for our children to grow to adulthood without enduring some damage to their emotions. Children suffer daily from peer pressure and are overcome by such negative emotions as rejection, guilt, anger, grief, low self-esteem and depression. Many get stuck emotionally at some level and never get beyond that stage into freedom, resulting in emotional problems later in adulthood. Some have reached out for love, approval, and affection as children, but they got a rejection, shame, and guilt.

Jesus promised His disciples in John 14:16-17 that He would ask the Father to give them a Helper (the Holy Spirit), who will be with them forever; and would not leave them as orphans. In other words, He is saying to you as a parent, "I will send you One (Holy Spirit, Helper, Comforter) whom you can call upon who will come alongside and help your family with their infirmities."

We have a great High Priest who does not just understand the fact of our infirmities; He understands the feeling of our infirmities. He understands the pain, frustrations, anxieties, hurts, feelings of abandonment, loneliness, isolation, rejection, and depression. He can do this because he has experienced all of these emotions. Knowing that the Lord is aware of those who suffer emotionally is a great source of comfort. In Hebrews 4:15, we read, *"For we do not have a high priest who cannot sympathise with our weaknesses, but One who was tempted in all things as we are, yet without sin."*

Words of Wisdom: God can turn bad things around to work together for your good. He can change hurtful things in your family into helpful things. Only the Holy Spirit truly knows the mind of God. And only the Holy Spirit truly understands our children. Because He understands the inside of them and the inside of God's heart, He knows how to get the two together. And so, *"The Spirit Himself intercedes for us with groanings too deep to be uttered." "For we do not know how to pray as we should, but the Spirit Himself intercedes for us" (Rom. 8:26).* Emotional healing takes place by the work of the Holy Spirit. The Holy Spirit, our Helper, will not only come alongside your family, but He also comes to work inside them.

Scripture Meditation: John 14:16-18 - AMP
And I will ask the Father, and He will give you another Helper (Comforter, Advocate, Intercessor—Counselor, Strengthener, Standby), to be with you forever— the Spirit of Truth, whom the

world cannot receive [and take to its heart] because it does not see Him or know Him, but you know Him because He (the Holy Spirit) remains with you continually and will be in you. "I will not leave you as orphans [comfortless, bereaved, and helpless]; I will come [back] to you.

Your Declaration: I declare that Jesus is Lord over my family and reigns over our emotions. I plead the blood of Jesus over my children's emotions. If they are battered and bruised emotionally, I proclaim the name of Jesus over their situation and circumstances. Lord Jesus, come into their hearts and bind up any brokenness. The Lord will restore health to my children and heal their wounds (Jer. 30:17). My family's emotion is held in check by the Word of God; thus, our response is always to accomplish God's will. I cast out any words, snares, and curses attached to my children because of emotional pain. They are children of Light (1 Thess. 5:5). God is Light, and darkness cannot overcome my family because we belong to Him (John 1:5). My children will not be afraid nor be dismayed, for the Lord God is with them as a mighty warrior, comforting them in times of pain, calming their fears and restoring hope (Deut 31:8). I bind demonic attacks affecting my children's sense of sight, smell, taste, touch and hearing. I bind all evil against their emotions and all evil against points of their body used by witchcraft. They are free from anxiety, panic attacks and depression and healed of all negative emotions welled up inside. Lord, remove any bitter feelings of anger and betrayal and enable them to stop thinking about painful memories of the past. I bind emotional attacks and trauma in any family member and loose our minds, will and emotions from every assignment of the spirits of darkness. We have the mind of Christ and think about things that are true, noble, things that are right, pure, lovely, admirable, excellent or praiseworthy (Phil. 4:8). We are strong and courageous. My children are not afraid or tremble in dread. Lord, help them to forgive those who have wronged them and not to harbour hatred. Please enable them to forgive those that have hurt and betrayed them. I plead the blood of Jesus over their minds, will and emotions. The son of God has set my family free, and we are free indeed (John 8:36). This is my prayer and declaration in Jesus' name.

PRAY FOR CHILDREN OF THE WORLD:

Ask the Lord to comfort them in times of pain, calm their fears and restore hope in their lives.

- WEEK 22 –

DECLARATIONS AGAINST BAD DREAMS / NIGHTMARES

As followers of Christ, we have the complete spiritual authority to demolish all the enemy's works against us when we pray in the name of Jesus. We must pray to forbid the operation of all demonic, wicked dreams, bind its assignment and break its hold and power over our lives. Deliverance begins when you cancel the negative effects of your dreams with the force of prayers through the power of the Word. Mark 3:27 says, "No man can enter into a strong man's house and spoil his goods, except he will first bind the strong man and then he will plunder his house." In James 4:7, the Bible instructs us to "Submit yourselves therefore to God. Resist the devil, and he will flee from you." Submission to God and resisting the enemy by the power in the name of Jesus is key to victory over dream attacks.

Tips for Understanding Your Children's Dreams:

1) Pay attention to repeated dreams: If your child has a repeated (similar) dream more than once or twice, you need to pay attention.

2) Write down the dreams: Don't despise your child's dreams because you don't understand them initially. Instead, write them in a notebook and pray for discernment. God may allow you to see deep things that will enforce their breakthrough as you pray about the dream.

3) Pray and nullify any bad dream. Rejoice, worship and thank God for good dreams, but ensure you take the authority, plead the blood of Jesus, and cancel any bad dreams. Ask the Holy Spirit for interpretation.

4) Keep a close eye on what your children are exposed to on television, social media, movies, and other forms of entertainment, as they might serve as portals through which demons can enter their dreams.

Words of Wisdom: If you or your child wake up from a bad dream, don't be afraid. Reassure your child not to be afraid. God did not give you a spirit of fear, He gave you a spirit of power to take authority over the nightmare by cancelling the dream. Cancel the negative dream, bind it from manifesting in the physical and forbid any assignment of the enemy. Cast the bad dream out of your lives and recover anything they stole from you in the name of Jesus. In Matthew 18:18, the Bible states that whatever we bind (declare illegal) on earth will be bound in heaven, and whatever we loose on earth will be loosed in heaven. Therefore, we must take authority and bind up the enemy's attacks on our children's sleep. Ask God to give them sweet, God-given dreams when they lay their head to rest. The Lord will destroy any plans that the enemy has for their sleep in the name of Jesus.

Scripture Meditation: Psalm 56:3

"Whenever I am afraid, I will trust in You."

Your Declaration: I declare that my family are covered under the shadow of God's mighty wings. In peace and with a tranquil heart, my family will lie down and sleep, for You alone, O Lord, make us dwell in safety and confident trust (Ps. 4:8). The Lord will cause the enemies who rise against my children in the dream to be defeated before their faces; they will come out against my children one way but flee before them seven ways (Deut. 28:7). I cancel bad dreams that would bring afflictions and diseases into my family and bind demonic attacks and arrows. Every evil, wicked plan of the enemy to unleash nightmares and demonic dreams shall not come to pass in our lives in the name of Jesus. The awful nightmares and night terrors my family have been experiencing are over. I bind any assignment of the enemy to feed my children in the dream. I plead the blood of Jesus on each child and speak peace over their sleep. They will not be afraid when they lie down, and their sleep will be sweet. They will not be afraid of sudden terror nor trouble from the wicked when it comes. (Prov. 3:24-25). I rebuke every demonic spirit and spiritual personality sent on assignment against my children's dream life and nullify their influences, attacks and manipulation in the name of Jesus. I bind up the attacks that the enemy has had on their sleep.

God has not given my children the spirit of fear, but of power, and love, and a sound mind (2 Tim. 1:7). I bind fear and anxiety in the mighty name of Jesus. No weapon formed against my family in the dream shall prosper! God is the strength of our hearts and our portion forever (Ps. 73:26). Bad dreams have no power over my family. We have good dreams and peaceful sleep. I rebuke any spirit of restlessness or insomnia in the name of Jesus and disconnect my family from wicked spiritual personalities of evil dreams and covenants in the name of Jesus. I sanctify our home, bedrooms and every place we lie down to sleep with the cleansing blood of Jesus Christ. As my family lie down to sleep, the light of Almighty God overshadows us and destroys every darkness around us. I take authority and plead the blood of Jesus over the atmosphere of our home environment, my children's school environment, university/college and workplace environment in the name of Jesus. I forbid and rebuke any oppressive spirit from having dominion over my family. I bind and put to flight every evil dream and Satanic gathering summoned concerning my children. I take authority against evil and Satanic arrows sent or fired at my children in the dream from the time they were born. I render you powerless and return you to the sender in the name of Jesus. I forbid nightmares and night terrors and bind their assignments in my children's dreams. I break the hold and power of all bad dreams and cast them out of my children's lives in the name of Jesus! I decree that my family are free from every form of bondage placed on our lives through demonic dreams. We shall not be victims of nightmares ever again. This is my prayer and declaration in Jesus' name.

PRAY FOR CHILDREN OF THE WORLD:
Pray that the light of Almighty God overshadows them and destroys every darkness in the name of Jesus.

DECLARATIONS AGAINST MIND ATTACKS

As God's children, we are frequently subjected to vicious attacks on our minds and emotions, and our children are no exception. Right now, the enemy is targeting the minds of our children and family. Did you know Satan is currently assaulting your child's mind? Undoubtedly, we are all targets for the enemy's schemes, but he is smart enough to recognise that attacks on our children are especially powerful. The greatest arena of spiritual warfare is the mind. The enemy assigns mind-binding spirits to steal our children's vision, destroy their joy, and take away their destinies. This spirit attacks many youths today. Mind-controlling spirits can enter through ungodly music, occult literature, pornography, false doctrine and religions, drugs, and apathy. Satan despises and seeks to destroy our children. We are at war! We must not be ignorant of the devil's devices, weapons, and strategies.

Is your child feeling sad, having self-doubt, depressed and having suicidal thoughts? It's the enemy attacking that child's mind! Satan is always after the mind. He is currently attempting to attack and destroy our world, focusing on our youth and the next generation. He is working tirelessly to conquer our children's minds, as the mind is the primary battlefield. He is serious about pursuing the next generation. The Bible says we must not be ignorant of the devil's devices or schemes. "...that no advantage may be gained over us by Satan; for we are not ignorant of his schemes." We must realise that, like it or not, we must fight and wage war for our children's lives on our knees if they are to survive the brutal mind attacks of the enemy.

When we think about what happened in Genesis 3 and how Eve was deceived, we realise that the cunning serpent whispered a thought to her, and she reasoned it out in her mind until it became acceptable to disobey God's command. In 2 Corinthians10:5, Paul instructs us to use our spiritual weapons to dismantle the arguments that the serpent has implanted in our minds. "For though we walk in the flesh, we do not war according to the flesh. For the weapons of our warfare are not carnal but mighty in God for pulling down strongholds, casting down arguments and every high thing that exalts itself against the knowledge of God, bringing every thought into captivity to the obedience of Christ," According to Paul, the weapons at our disposal are mighty through God, not just to get by, but also to demolish these strongholds! So fight your battles with God's powerful weapons of warfare, tearing down the enemy's strongholds so that your children will not fall into his trap in Jesus' name.

Words of Wisdom: God adores your children wholeheartedly. They are the crowning glory of His creation, and He does not want them to perish. However, the devil despises God and his creation. I pray that God will deliver your children from that single thought that leads them astray. They will not accept negative thoughts implanted in their minds by the enemy in the name of Jesus. I pray that your children will not take and act on evil thoughts. They will reject thoughts that cause them to say and do harmful and destructive things to others. If the devil controls your child's mind, he has complete control over their life. I encourage you to fight his lies with the truth of God's Word to win this battle for your children's minds. Do it in Jesus' way, and you will have spiritual victory in Jesus' name!

Scripture Meditation: 2 Corinthians 10:3-5 (AMP)

"For though we walk in the flesh [as mortal men], we are not carrying on our [spiritual] warfare according to the flesh and using the weapons of man. The weapons of our warfare are not physical [weapons of flesh and blood]. Our weapons are divinely powerful for the destruction of fortresses. We are destroying sophisticated arguments and every exalted and proud thing that sets itself up against the [true] knowledge of God, and we are taking every thought and purpose captive to the obedience of Christ."

Your Declaration: I declare that Satan's thoughts will not establish a foothold in my children's lives. His lies will not be able to bind the minds of my children or keep them trapped in a place of sickness, suffering, torment, bitterness, or unforgiveness. I command every spirit that binds the mind to depart from my children's lives in the name of Jesus. The enemy will not deter them from discovering the truth in the Word of God. I destroy the enemy's strongholds, evil imaginations that Satan plants in their minds and any other thoughts that exalt themselves against the knowledge of God. I cast out of my children's minds all spirits of control, witchcraft, mind-binding, confusion, double-mindedness, mental bondage, madness, insanity, fantasy, passivity, knowledge block, intellectualism, ignorance, lust, and evil thinking in the name of Jesus. I loose their minds from any mental bondage and command every mind-binding spirit to go in the name of Jesus! I rebuke you lying demon in the name of Jesus! Get thee hence! I decree that my children have a sound mind. They think Godly thoughts, imagine Godly imaginations and dream Godly dreams. My children have the mind of Christ (Phil. 2:5). I henceforth declare that my children are set free from any mind-controlling spirits that may have been affecting them. Their thoughts have been set free! The peace of God, which passes all understanding, will guard my children's hearts and minds through Christ Jesus (Phil. 4:7). I plead the blood of Jesus over my children's minds. This is my prayer and declaration in Jesus' name.

PRAY FOR CHILDREN OF THE WORLD:
Pray that the Lord will deliver them from mind binding spirits and the enemy will not keep them from the truth of God's Word.

- WEEK 24 –

DECLARATIONS AGAINST WITCHCRAFT ATTACKS

Satan's domain is witchcraft, and one of his specialities is imitating God's work. The devil uses witchcraft as one of the most lethal and destructive powers he wields against humankind. In Exodus 8:7, when Moses performed miracles in front of Pharaoh, the magicians at the time achieved the same things by the power of the devil. The enemy's use of witchcraft is one of the most dangerous weapons at his disposal. He specialises in manipulating people, exercising control, and killing them. Every time you observe manipulation, a witchcraft attack occurs in the background. Are members of your family or friends trying to exert influence over your spouse or child? Is it possible that they are getting out of hand? This is an attempt to harm your family through witchcraft. Witchcraft hides behind the veil to carry out evil deeds. They don't assault you or your family in the open; instead, they hide behind a veil so you can't see them.

Jesus said, "The thief does not come except to steal, and to kill, and to destroy. I have come that they may have life and that they may have it more abundantly." (John 10:10). According to what Jesus says here, the thief comes to your life with the intent to kill, steal, and destroy anything and all that is good in your home and family. The burglar has arrived to rob you of your family and home! He intends to ruin not just your career but also your joy, peace, health and well-being, finances, relationship, and children.

The thief's only goal is to make a mess of anything he can steal and get his hands on. Any manipulation, including witchcraft, weakens, dominates, and ultimately destroys families and homes. Satan is incredibly cunning, and we must be careful never to give him power over our household. It is time to rise and pray against the forces of darkness in the lives of our families. The Lord will deliver and protect your family from every plan of evil in the name of Jesus. "And from the days of John the Baptist until now the kingdom of heaven suffers violence, and the violent take it by force" (Matthew 11:12). I plead the blood of Jesus against any arrows of witchcraft directed against your family and pray for a hedge of protection around each member of your household in Jesus name.

Words of Wisdom: As you raise your children, you will face challenges in your walk with the Lord. Your family will go through times when the devil will push their emotional buttons to keep them low and depressed. Sometimes, the enemy will try to get you or your family off track or make you give up on your walk with Christ. But when these witchcraft attacks happen, tell the devil to be quiet and tell him he can't give you evil thoughts. Tell him to get out of your way! Tell him you won't believe his terrible news or lies, so he might as well go elsewhere. You're no longer a pushover! You know how he does things now, and you're determined that he won't steal, kill, or destroy one more good thing from your family in the name of Jesus. God will always keep all kinds of evil away from your family and protect you. Therefore, you must resist the devil, and he will flee from your home!

Scripture Meditation: Psalm 121:7-8 (AMP)

"The LORD will protect you from all evil; He will keep your life. The LORD will guard your going out and your coming in [everything that you do] from this time forth and forever."

Your Declaration: I declare that Jesus has fully disarmed principalities and powers and has delivered my family from the forces of darkness. My children are delivered out of the hand of wicked and unreasonable men (2 Thess 3:2). All witches and wizards who seek after the lives of my children and family will be put to shame and brought to dishonour. Those who plot our hurt are turned back and brought to confusion. They are blown away like chaff before the wind, with the angel of the Lord pursuing them (Ps. 35:4-6). Let the net they have hidden catch them, into that very destruction let them fall (Ps. 35:8). The Lord is faithful, who will establish my family and guard us from the evil one (2 Thess. 3:3). We are preserved for God's heavenly Kingdom (2 Tim. 4:18). No weapon formed against my family shall prosper in the name of Jesus (Ps. 54:17). When the enemy comes in like a flood, the Spirit of the Lord will lift up a standard against him (Isa. 59:19). My children are free from every attack of witchcraft, sorcery and divination in the name of Jesus. I command the agenda of the wicked to be frustrated in their lives. The hammer of the wicked is broken. Every coven of witches where my name or my children's names are taken shall be consumed by the fire of God, in the name of Jesus (Heb. 12:29). I command all spirits of witchcraft and divination to come out in the name of Jesus. I break the power of divination, deception, seduction, sorcery and intimidation over my family. I break all curses, hexes, spells, incantations, and powers - and through the Blood of the Lamb - destroy the works of witches, warlocks, wizards, sorcerers and all other powers of darkness assigned against my family. I bind demonic activity and declare null and void all forms of voodoo, jinxes, potions, bewitchments, death and destruction. I release the fire of the Holy Spirit to consume and destroy every hidden activity of witchcraft in my children's lives (Heb. 12:29). Who shall bring a charge against God's elect? It is God who has justified my family (Rom. 8:33). If God is for us, who can be against us? (Romans 8:31). The devil's works shall not prosper against my family. This is my prayer and declaration in Jesus' name.

PRAY FOR CHILDREN OF THE WORLD:

Pray they are delivered out of the hand of wicked and unreasonable men.

- WEEK 25 –

DECLARATIONS AGAINST GENERATIONAL CURSES

In today's society, curses are still placed on some Christian families, and those curses continue to have an effect. Many Christian households require deliverance from curses spoken against them before they were converted to Christianity or from curses brought upon them due to their participation in practices such as witchcraft and idolatry. Disobedience to the Word of God and sin are the root causes of family curses, which are then visited upon those families. Curses are released when someone breaks God's laws. "All the nations will say, "Why has the Lord done this thing to this land? Why this great outburst of anger?" Then people will say, "It is because they abandoned (broke) the covenant of the Lord, the God of their fathers, which He made with them when He brought them out of the land of Egypt. For they went and served other gods and worshipped them, [false] gods whom they have not known and whom He had not allotted (given) to them. So the anger of the Lord burned against this land, bringing on it every curse that is written in this book; and the Lord uprooted them from their land in anger and in wrath and in great indignation, and cast them into another land, as it is this day" (Deuteronomy 29:24-28 - AMP). We can conclude that the curse was a form of retribution for sin. As a result, a generational curse is punishment for sin that is passed down through generations. The consequences of sin are inevitably passed down from generation to generation.

When a parent leads an immoral lifestyle, his children are more likely to follow in his footsteps. The verse from the book of Exodus 20:5 seems to imply that future generations will deliberately choose to carry on the crimes of their parents. Children who grow up in homes with physical or emotional abuse have a greater risk of becoming violent adults. Those who had parents who misused alcohol are at a greater risk of abusing alcohol themselves. The same reasoning applies to sexual immorality and any other evil a person might commit. This text talks about "rebellious children" and "ungodly fathers." Therefore, it is not unfair for God to punish sin up to the third or fourth generation because people in those generations continue to commit the same sins as their predecessors.

The power of prayer can destroy any curse! So let us pray that our children will not make the same mistakes our forefathers did. Every curse passed down through the generations must be broken in the name of Jesus!

Words of Wisdom: Remember that the devil is the one who fell, and since we have authority over him, we have no reason to fear him. As long as we exercise faith and use our authority over him, he cannot harm us. Through the blood of Jesus Christ, our Lord, we have power over all curses and break them in Jesus name.

Scripture Meditation: Luke 10:18-20 (AMP)
"He said to them, "I watched Satan fall from heaven like [a flash of] lightning. Listen carefully: I have given you authority [that you now possess] to tread on serpents and scorpions, and [the ability to exercise authority] over all the power of the enemy (Satan); and

nothing will [in any way] harm you. Nevertheless do not rejoice at this, that the spirits are subject to you, but rejoice that your names are recorded in heaven."

Your Declaration: I declare that no curse over my family can stand because Christ has redeemed us from the curse of the law, being made a curse for our sake (Gal 3:13). Therefore, we have dominion over generational and territorial curses. Lord, forgive my family for any known or unknown sin that may give the enemy legal ground to afflict us. I renounce and repent of any sin that may have opened my family up for curses to operate. I cover myself and my family with the blood of Jesus. I break the curse of hell and death over our lives in the name of Jesus. None of my family shall die prematurely. I break all curses of sickness and death. We shall not die before our time; instead, we shall live and declare the works of the Lord. I break the hold and power of every curse bringing affliction into my family. I break the curse of failure and lack of progress and command it to lose my family in the name of Jesus. I bind all curses operating in our lives ten generations back and break their hold and power in the name of Jesus. I break every curse of damnation spoken over our bloodline; I take authority and trample on serpents and scorpions and over all the power of the enemy working against my family (Luke 10:19). These curses have no effect on my children or myself in the name of Jesus. We are loosed from all generational curses and hereditary spirits. We are loosed from the bonds of wickedness and oppression (Isa 58:6). I command all demons to leave my family right now in the name of Jesus (Mark 7:29). By the power in the blood of Jesus Christ, I break the yoke of every curse that has come to my family through rituals or ritual sacrifice. I break the power of every curse that has come into my family through transfer by another human being. I break every generational curse of witchcraft over my family in the name of Jesus! I declare every curse ceases to operate in our lives and cast out the demons behind it in the name of Jesus. All curses of failure, lack, debt, sickness and poverty are broken in the name of Jesus. The Word of God declares there is no sorcery against Jacob, nor any divination against Israel (Num. 23:23). We are the seed of Abraham. No curse from today can touch us, and no witchcraft spell has power over us in the awesome name of Jesus Christ. This is my prayer and declaration in Jesus' name.

PRAY FOR CHILDREN OF THE WORLD:

Pray that all curses of failure, lack, debt, sickness and poverty are broken.

DECLARATIONS IN TIMES OF TROUBLE

Adversity is a part of every family's journey. Yet, sometimes we are at a loss for words when praying for our broken families. When things are tough, we can find comfort when turning to the Bible, which is densely populated with words of wisdom, encouragement, and motivation to get through the tough times. One of the children may be struggling with substance abuse or alcoholism; others may be struggling with self-harm or mental illness; others may struggle with exams, relationships, and peer pressure; and others may be incarcerated. Yet, the Bible gives us hope that despite our difficulties, nothing will be able to separate us from God's love demonstrated in Christ Jesus, our Saviour.

"No, in all these things we are more than conquerors through him who loved us. For I am sure that neither death nor life, nor angels nor rulers, nor things present nor things to come, nor powers, nor height nor depth, nor anything else in all creation, will be able to separate us from the love of God in Christ Jesus our Lord." — Romans 8:37-39

Job is one of the great instances in the Bible of people who proved that with God as your guide, you could go through terrible circumstances and come out on the other side. Job had everything that anyone in his time would want: a large family, a great business, good health, and a lot of money, yet he lost it all!

Yet, he trusted God despite not understanding why he had to endure so much struggle and loss. During his anguish, his friends argued with him and accused him of sin, claiming that his suffering was God's retribution. Finally, he humbled himself before God and acknowledged that trusting God in the midst of it all was sufficient.

"The Lord also will be a refuge for the oppressed, a refuge in times of trouble." – (Psalm 9:9)

Are you or your child presently experiencing a challenging situation for which you have no explanation? I encourage you to trust God in all circumstances and stay consistent in your faith, no matter the situation. Psalm 46:1 - *"God is our refuge and strength, a very present help in trouble."*

Words of Wisdom: Are your children giving you trouble? Even when you don't understand, I encourage you to trust in God's wisdom. Although you may never know why bad things are happening in your family right now, trusting in God will help you move forward in the best way. I encourage you to rely upon His Word even in adversity. Don't forget to ask Him for help. While it is tempting to look for earthly solutions during difficult times, God is capable of assisting you and your family in ways you could never imagine. I pray that God will give you the strength to keep praying and standing in faith, believing and trusting in His Word, as you go through this hard time. God can help you get through anything. Nothing is impossible with Him. Remain patient, don't give up and don't lose hope.

Scripture Meditation: Proverbs 3:5-6 (AMP)

"Trust in and rely confidently on the Lord with all your heart and do not rely on your own insight or understanding. In all your ways know and acknowledge and recognize Him, and He will make your paths straight and smooth [removing obstacles that block your way]."

Your Declaration: I declare that trouble will not overwhelm my family. The enemy's flame will not kindle upon us and the gates of hell will not prevail against us. When we pass through the waters, the Lord will be with us, and through the rivers, we will not be overwhelmed. When we walk through the fire, we will not be scorched, nor will the flame burn us (Isa. 43:2). The Lord will trouble all those who trouble our lives and destinies, and recompense tribulations upon them (2 Thess. 1:6). Every mountain of trouble in my children's way shall become a plain in the name of Jesus (Zech. 4:7). I plead the blood of Jesus against all demons assigned to cause trouble in my children's lives at school, at college, at university, workplace or in nursery or kindergarten/childminder. The Lord our God in our midst, the Mighty One, will save my family from trouble. He will rejoice over my children with gladness; He will quiet them with His love and rejoice over them with singing (Zeph. 3:17). They overcome every obstacle at school, at work, at college, at university, outlast every challenge and come through every difficulty. They scale every wall of adversity and overcome every trial sent against their lives by the enemy. All crooked places in my family are made straight, and all the valleys exalted in the name of Jesus. The Lord of hosts is with us; the God of Jacob is our refuge from trouble (Ps. 46:7). I bind all demonic assignments to cause trouble between myself, my children and other members of the family. I bind and rebuke any trouble between them and their friends, between them and their colleagues and other agents of evil. In the name of Jesus, I release the Lord's power and authority over all devils that my family encounters.(Matt. 10:1). The Lord has commanded victories for my family. We are saved from our enemies, and those who hate us are put to shame (Ps. 44:7). This is my prayer and declaration in Jesus' name.

PRAY FOR CHILDREN OF THE WORLD:

That the gates and plans of hell will not prevail against them.

- WEEK 27 -

DECLARATIONS
FOR PEACE

The world is in chaos, but we don't have to be anxious or afraid. Our world craves peace but finds it elusive. We need peace in these difficult times. In John 14, shortly before Jesus was crucified, He talked to His disciples. He knows their hearts would be troubled, but He promises them a spirit of peace. Although He would leave them, He promised to comfort them, "Peace I leave with you; My [perfect] peace I give to you; not as the world gives do I give to you. Do not let your heart be troubled, nor let it be afraid. [Let My perfect peace calm you in every circumstance and give you courage and strength for every challenge.]." (John 14: 27 - AMP)

The peace that Jesus brings extends to all members of our family. The Lord's deep desire for us, His followers and the world in general is to know His peace and joy, even in times of trouble. No matter the struggle that is before you, God has an answer. He has good in store for you and your children. There will be hardships, challenges, and pain in this life, but they don't always last. Be at peace when you feel overwhelmed with family issues and struggle to find peace. The Lord is watching out for you and your family. Isaiah 26:3 states, "You will keep in perfect and constant peace the one whose mind is steadfast [that is, committed and focused on You—in both inclination and character], because he trusts and takes refuge in You [with hope and confident expectation]."

Trust in the Lord; He will not disappoint you. Peace comes because He is the Prince of peace!

Words of Wisdom: To know God is to experience His peace. The nearer we move to God, the more of His peace we can experience. We come into God's presence through His Son, Jesus Christ, who has already paid the price for our sins. Through Him alone do we have peace with God. When we stay in constant communion with God, we can remain peaceful - even in the midst of trouble. When our children develop a lifestyle of making the Lord their refuge, they begin to live in the peace of God.

Scripture Meditation: Colossians 3:15 NIV
"Let the peace of Christ rule in your hearts, since as members of one body you were called to peace. And be thankful."

Your Declaration: I declare that God surrounds my family with the peace of Christ. God's kindness shall not depart from us, nor shall His covenant of peace be removed from our lives (Isa. 54:10). We always have peace, and God is with us (2 Thess. 3:16). My children possess the peace of Christ, which surpasses all understanding. The Lord is their peace in the storm. They remain calm in chaotic situations. Their focus is steady on the Lord, and they shall not be moved by fear. They shall not be troubled or afraid but will trust in God because they have His peace like a river. The peace of God, which passes all understanding, will guard the hearts and minds of my family in Christ Jesus (Phil. 4:7). We shall not be a prey for the nations, nor shall beasts of the land devour us, but we shall dwell safely, and no one shall make us afraid (Ezek. 34:28). The Lord will keep my family in perfect and constant peace, for our mind stays on Him (Isaiah 26:3). The Lord shall teach all my children, and great shall be their peace (Isaiah 54:13). The peace of God which passes all understanding encompasses their hearts and minds in Christ Jesus. Therefore, since my children and I are justified by faith, we have peace with God through our Lord Jesus Christ (Romans 5:1). This is my prayer and declaration in Jesus' name.

PRAY FOR CHILDREN OF THE WORLD:
That they shall not be a prey for the Nations. God will shine His face on them and give them peace.

DECLARATIONS AGAINST INTERNET/SOCIAL MEDIA ADDICTION

Insomuch as social media can be a tremendous social network tool, we cannot overlook its evils in our society. Its effects on our children can be dangerous, so it should be of particular importance to us as parents to pray for our children not to get sucked into the web. Children who spend more time on social media become victims of depression and anxiety because it adversely affects their mood and thought processes. It is among the leading causes of sleep deprivation in youths of today. They are constantly worried about what their friends post and share and can stay active on social media for longer durations if not prompted to stop. Uncontrolled social media usage can lead to Internet addiction. The more time our children spend on social media, the more they become exposed to feeds, stories and ideas they want to explore. This obsession could eventually become an addiction that, if not handled early, can affect their mental health, school performance, and personal development. Internet consumption affects children in a big way, and social media is a large part of that. Like anything else we overuse or come to rely on, our children can become so dependent on social media and end up with an obsession they cannot break. They could be cyberbullied or end up in a dangerous situation. I pray that social media will not become an idol in our children's lives in the name of Jesus.

Words of Wisdom: The Bible urges us to set our hearts on things above, not earthly things that consume the world. *"Since, then, you have been raised with Christ, set your hearts on things above, where Christ is, seated at the right hand of God. Set your minds on things above, not on earthly things." (Col. 3:1-2 – NIV).* After scrolling on a social media site, we can see how easy it is to fix our thoughts and heart on things in the world that are not godly. Let us pray and consider how God wants our children to be using social media and keep a watch to see if they are spending too much time on their phones and other devices. Becoming obsessed and addicted to anything or anyone is dangerous to their health and wellbeing. When they become addicted or obsessed with social media, they essentially make it an idol by putting it before God.

Scripture Meditation: Exodus 20:2-6

"I am the LORD your God, who brought you out of the land of Egypt, out of the house of bondage. "You shall have no other gods before Me. "You shall not make for yourself a carved image—any likeness of anything that is in heaven above, or that is in the earth beneath, or that is in the water under the earth; you shall not bow down to them nor serve them. For I, the LORD your God, am a jealous God, visiting the iniquity of the fathers upon the children to the third and fourth generations of those who hate Me, but showing mercy to thousands, to those who love Me and keep My commandments."

Your Declaration: I declare that whatever my family do on social media, we do for the glory of God (1 Cor. 10:31). The enemy will not groom my children through deception or lead them into temptation through social media. They will not prioritise social media over their work or spiritual growth in Christ. They will not lose job opportunities because of social media addiction and will not waste valuable time and money on the Internet. They will follow Jesus and not the world around them. They will not be lost or destroyed through social media. Their hearts will not be hard or insensitive to the will of God. They walk as children of light and have no fellowship with the unfruitful works of darkness. Their hearts are fixed on things above, not on earthly things that consume the world. My children are delivered from the lust of the eyes, the lust of the flesh and the pride of life. They will not look with approval on anything vile on the Internet or take part in anything crooked. They set their minds on things above, not on things on the earth (Col. 3:2). They are not addicted to getting likes, becoming caught up or worrying about what other people think of them. They will not compare themselves to others. They will not depend on social media likes and followers to define their worth, feel wanted or be loved. They will not be addicted to social media and end up with an obsession. Instead, they will use their social media account to share the love of Jesus. Nothing and no one will distract or separate my family from the love of God. We will spend more time with God instead of wasting time on social media. I take authority and plead the blood of Jesus over my children's minds to protect against infiltration from end-time mind control. No weapon of the enemy formed or fashioned against my family shall prosper (Isa. 54:17). We are covered by the blood of Jesus. This is my prayer and declaration in Jesus' name.

PRAY FOR CHILDREN OF THE WORLD:

Pray that the enemy will not groom them through social media. Instead, they will follow Jesus and not the world around them.

DECLARATIONS AGAINST ADDICTION TO PORNOGRAPHY

Did you know that the average age of first exposure to pornography is 9 to 11 years old? It is not a matter of if your child will encounter pornography, but when. Your family is being targeted online! This statement is not to sound alarmist; rather, it reminds us that our children depend on us to protect them. A daily pornographic internet search is performed by approximately 33% of males aged 16 to 34. Teens are the most vulnerable age group to watch pornographic content, and Christians are not exempt from this. We find it easy to think that the problem is "out there," somewhere on the other side of the church walls; however, pornography has become a major problem within the Body of Christ due to its ease of access. I mention this because it's easy to believe that the problem is "out there." When we were younger, it was not nearly as easy for people to watch pornographic movies as it is now. Back then, people had to go out of their way to find it, and they often did so in shady stores where they didn't want to be seen. Today, you only need to click a few times on your smartphone, iPad, or computer. Our desire for sin inevitably leads us to sin. There is, however, hope.

Our sinful nature makes it easy to engage in sexual immorality, masturbation, and pornography. Those who expose themselves to temptations agree in silence with Satan's lies and live defeated lives due to their inability to refrain from sinning. As parents, it is our responsibility to familiarise ourselves with various social media platforms so that we can make educated choices regarding the types of mobile applications (apps) we will let our young children use and how they can do so securely. We must recognise the dangers of the pornographic epidemic.

Words of Wisdom: Satan drives the sinful nature if the mind is not filled with God's words daily. *"... what a man sows, he will reap" (Ga. 6:7).* Your children are in God's good hands. He desires for them to turn away from pornography, and he will assist them if we continue to pray and fast without ceasing.

Scripture Meditation: 1 Corinthians 6:18-20 (AMP)
"Run away from sexual immorality [in any form, whether thought or behaviour, whether visual or written]. Every other sin that a man commits is outside the body, but the one who is sexually immoral sins against his own body. Do you not know that your body is a temple of the Holy Spirit who is within you, whom you have [received as a gift] from God, and that you are not your own [property]? You were bought with a price [you were actually purchased with the precious blood of Jesus and made His own]. So then, honour and glorify God with your body."

Your Declaration: I declare that my family has overcome the world through the power of the Holy Spirit. My children will experience the blessing of their sexuality under the protection of God's heavenly standard as they walk in the light. They are set free from the spirit of the world, the lust of the flesh, the lust of the eyes, and the pride of life (1 John 2:16). They avoid any form of sexual immorality, whether it be thought or behaviour, visual or written. They walk in the Spirit and will not satisfy their fleshly desires. I cast out and loose my children from any spirits of pornography and bind all spirits of fantasy and lustful thinking in the name of Jesus. I cast out and loose my family from any spirit spouses. I command all hereditary spirits of lust from both sides of our family to leave in the name of Jesus. My children glorify God in their bodies. They flee from sexual immorality (1 Cor. 6:18). They do not allow sin to reign in their body or submit to its lust (Romans 6:12). They present their bodies to the Lord as a holy, acceptable living sacrifice. I break all curses of perversion put on my children by spirits of witchcraft that work with lust and command them to leave in the name of Jesus. My children do not conform to the spirit of the world, but God's Word renews their minds daily. I command all spirits of pornography to come out of their appetite in the name of Jesus. They will not engage in prostitution. I now declare that my children are free of bondage to pornography, and I sever every soul-tie that this evil addiction has created. Sin shall not have dominion over my family. This is my prayer and declaration in Jesus' name.

PRAY FOR CHILDREN OF THE WORLD:

Pray they are delivered from all addictions to pornography and are not groomed by sexual predators or trafficked for sexual exploitation.

DECLARATIONS FOR HEALING & HEALTH.

We see numerous examples of Jesus healing the sick throughout the New Testament. He performed miracles by touching, healing, and transforming lives. One of the reasons Jesus healed the sick was to demonstrate that He possessed the power to restore health. In Matthew 8, we see Jesus heal a leper, a paralyzed man, and Peter's sick mother-in-law. He healed many others who were sick and oppressed by demons. "When evening had come, they brought to Him many who were demon-possessed. And He cast out the spirits with a word and healed all who were sick" (Matt. 8:16). His powerful healings demonstrate great love and compassion for humanity. Jesus forgives all our sins and heals all our diseases. *"And when Jesus went out, He saw a great multitude; and He was moved with compassion for them and healed their sick" (Matt. 14:14).* He is the One who sympathizes with us in our weakness and has sufficient power to remove our pain and suffering. As God's children, we have access to His healing power. He is our physician, assuring us that he will protect us from the awful diseases that plague this world. He healed everyone who asked, "according to their faith."

"Then He touched their eyes, saying, "According to your faith, let it be to you. And their eyes were opened" (Matt. 9:29-30). Healing people was important to Jesus then; it is still important to Him now.

Is anyone sick in your family or oppressed by demons? Jesus is willing to heal the sick. *"And whatever we ask we receive from Him, because we keep His commandments and do those things that are pleasing in His sight"* (1 John 3:22). Ask for your children's healing by faith, and indeed, He will answer! When we pray to Jesus and ask for His assistance, we can be confident that He hears us and will heal us. It is reassuring to know that God sees and cares for us, as He does not wish for any family member to suffer and is always looking out for our best interests. He offered Himself as a sacrifice for the remission of our sins, and it is by His stripes that we are healed. *"But He was wounded for our transgressions, He was bruised for our iniquities; the chastisement for our peace was upon Him, and by His stripes we are healed"* (Isa. 53:5).

Words of Wisdom: Encourage your child to put their complete trust in God for healing. Jesus is always available and prepared to comfort your family in His healing arms when they feel injured or need His divine healing touch for their physical body.

Scripture Meditation: Matthew 4:23-24

"And Jesus went about all Galilee, teaching in their synagogues, preaching the gospel of the kingdom, and healing all kinds of sickness and all kinds of disease among the people. Then His fame went throughout all Syria; and they brought to Him all sick people who were afflicted with various diseases and torments, and those who were demon-possessed, epileptics, and paralytics; and He healed them. Great multitudes followed Him—from Galilee, and from Decapolis, Jerusalem, Judea, and beyond the Jordan."

Your Declaration: I declare my family shall not die, but live and declare the works of the Lord (Ps. 118:17). Christ Jesus has redeemed us from the curse of the law; therefore, sickness, disease, pain, suffering, infirmity, poverty and spiritual death have no power over my household (Gal. 3:13). The Lord has healed all our diseases and redeemed our lives from destruction. He crowns my family with His lovingkindness and tender mercies (Ps. 103:3-4). We are redeemed from the curse of sickness, and by the stripes of Jesus, we are healed (1 Peter 2:24). In the name of Jesus, I bind the spirit of infirmity from operating in my home and family. Jesus took our sickness and carried our pain. No illness or affliction will come near my children and my home in the name of Jesus (Ps. 91:10). The blood of Jesus strengthens my children's immune system. Each member of my family is healed and delivered from all pain. Our healing springs forth speedily (Isa. 58:8). We prosper and walk in perfect health even as our soul prospers (3 John 2). My children are fearfully and wonderfully made (Ps. 139:14). God's strength is made perfect in their weakness, so when my children are weak, then they are strong (2 Cor. 12:9-10). All organs in their body function the way God intended. The Lord will fulfil the number of their days. He will bless their bread and their water and remove all sickness from their body (Ex. 23:25). I prophesy Ezekiel 37:9, Thus says the Lord GOD: Come from the four winds, O breath, and breathe on every organ in my children's body in the name of Jesus. I speak to every sickness and command it to leave now! I command all spirits of disease and infirmity to come out of my family in the name of Jesus! The Lord will satisfy us with long life and show us His salvation (Ps. 91:16). I break demonic curses of sickness and disease and command all inherited illnesses to leave my children's bodies in the name of Jesus. This is my prayer and declaration in Jesus' name.

PRAY FOR CHILDREN OF THE WORLD:

Children suffering from cancer, babies and children with disabilities.

Children with Autism and mental health challenges, children in hospital.

- WEEK 31 -

DECLARATIONS
OF OBEDIENCE

In Noah's day, the Bible tells us that wickedness had grown to such an extent on the earth that the Lord was sorry He had ever created humanity. *"The Lord saw that the wickedness (depravity) of man was great on the earth, and that every imagination or intent of the thoughts of his heart were only evil continually. The Lord regretted that He had made mankind on the earth, and He was [deeply] grieved in His heart"* (Genesis 6: 5-6).

Evil grew to such an extent that God decided to wipe the human race from the face of the earth, resulting from sin and disobedience. Disobedience grieves the heart of God. "So the Lord said, *"I will destroy (annihilate) mankind whom I have created from the surface of the earth—not only man, but the animals and the crawling things and the birds of the air—because it [deeply] grieves Me [to see mankind's sin] and I regret that I have made them"* (Genesis 6: 7).

It was a very sad time, but then the Lord looked and saw Noah! He saw Noah's heart of submission to His will. *"Noah was a righteous man [one who was just and had right standing with God], blameless in his [evil] generation; Noah walked (lived) [in habitual fellowship] with God"* (Genesis 6: 9). Because of obedience, the Bible notes that "Noah found favour and grace in the eyes of the Lord."

Instead of conforming to the evil of the society around him, Noah upheld morality and goodness. His obedience resulted in him and his entire family being saved from the flood that destroyed every other living thing on earth. Anyone who wants to know God and walk closely with Him must obey Him.

Our families are called to a life of obedience. Jesus calls us to follow and obey. Without obedience to God, we cannot walk fully in the blessing and enjoy the communion that our spirits desire.

Words of Wisdom: Noah walked in fellowship and obedience to God instead of conforming to the wickedness of the civilization around him. He lived amongst a rebellious and stubborn generation, a corrupt, absolutely depraved—spiritually and morally putrid society, but surrendered his heart with humility in habitual fellowship with God. As a result, he and every member of his family were saved from destruction. The actual worship of God begins with surrender. We cannot claim to love God without obeying Him and His Word. Obedience to God opens the door of His blessings to us and keeps us in His will. I pray your family will not conform to the evil of this world but walk in humility and habitual fellowship with God.

Scripture Meditation: Isaiah 1: 18-20

"Come now, and let us reason together," says the Lord, "Though your sins are like scarlet, they shall be as white as snow; though they are red like crimson, They shall be as wool. If you are willing and obedient, you shall eat the good of the land; but if you refuse and rebel, you shall be devoured by the sword"; for the mouth of the Lord has spoken."

Your Declaration: I declare that my family will observe the requirements of the Lord to walk in all His ways, to keep His statutes, His commandments, His judgements, His testimonies so that we may prosper in all that we do and wherever we turn (1 Kings 2:3). My children will faithfully obey the Lord, they will not refuse and rebel. They will diligently obey God's voice and carefully observe all His commandments (Deut. 28:1). My family shall love the Lord, be obedient to His voice and keep His covenant, then we shall be God's own special possession and treasure from among all peoples of the world. We shall be unto God a kingdom of priests and a holy nation set apart for His purpose (Ex. 19:5-6). My children no longer conform to the pattern of this world but are being transformed daily by the renewing of their minds (Rom. 12:2). They will not allow the world to squeeze them into its mould. They will walk in fellowship and obedience to God. They will not be pressured into following the corrupt customs, ungodly principles, or evil plans of action promoted by ungodly men. They will not walk in step with the wicked or stand in the way that sinners take or sit in the company of mockers. Their delight is in the law of the Lord, and on His law they meditate day and night (Ps. 1:1-2). My children will obey me as a parent in the Lord. They will accept my guidance and discipline as God's representative in the home. They will honour me as their parent and be respectful and obedient, that it may be well with them and that they may have a long life on earth (Eph. 6:1-3). This is my prayer and declaration in Jesus' name.

PRAY FOR CHILDREN OF THE WORLD:

That they walk in obedience to the will of God.

- WEEK 32 –

DECLARATIONS AGAINST REBELLION

Youth today are rebellious and disobedient to authority in our society. Our young people want to be the god of their lives, do their own thing and not care about walking in righteousness, and the Bible describes disobedience as equal to witchcraft because it makes God angry. Rebellion at its root is nothing more than deliberately choosing to be led by another spirit, a spirit of rebellion. It is choosing to do the enemy's will in direct opposition to that of God's will. In the Bible, Samuel said: *"Has the Lord as great delight in burnt offerings and sacrifices, as in obeying the voice of the Lord? Behold, to obey is better than sacrifice, and to heed than the fat of rams. For rebellion is as the sin of witchcraft, and stubbornness is like iniquity and idolatry. Because you have rejected the Word of the Lord, He also has rejected you from being king." (1 Sam. 15:22-23)*

In the account of Samson and Delilah, it would have been better had Samson been obedient to God's words, warnings, and commandments from the start. Instead, Samson wilfully chose to be led by another spirit. Although he eventually humbled himself, repented, and sacrificed his life in the end to defeat the Philistines, his rebellion cost him everything. His blessings, calling, anointing, and eventually, his very life. The seed of rebellion is germinating deep within every human heart. Rebelling against God's will and Word is a dangerous thing to do! There are dire consequences to rejecting the Word of the Lord. I pray that our children and family will not rebel against the will and Word of God, and the Holy Spirit will convict them and expose the truth to them in the name of Jesus.

Words of Wisdom: If we want to be victorious in the struggle against rebellion, we need to seek the Holy Spirit and rely on Him more than we do on our flesh and the reactions that come naturally to us. If a family member is walking in rebellion against God, it is not too late to intervene. Our God is merciful. I advise that we get down on our knees and ask the Lord's forgiveness. Let us ask Him to have mercy on our family. If possible, walk inside your child's room, pray the below declarations and anoint the room. Pray over their possessions. Lean on the Holy Spirit; He will guide and lead you.

Scripture Meditation: Ephesians 6:12-13 (AMP)
"For our struggle is not against flesh and blood [contending only with physical opponents], but against the rulers, against the powers, against the world forces of this [present] darkness, against the spiritual forces of wickedness in the heavenly (supernatural) places. Therefore, put on the complete Armor of God, so that you will be able to [successfully] resist and stand your ground in the evil day [of danger], and having done everything [that the crisis demands], to stand firm [in your place, fully prepared, immovable, victorious]."

Your Declaration: I declare that my family say no to sin and yes to the Lord. We take our stand against Satan and all his lying ways. My children obey God rather than men (Acts 5:29). I break the yoke of rebellion, stubbornness, pride and haughtiness in my family in the name of Jesus. There is no rebellion in my children. They are loosed from the yoke of rebellion. They are united in Christ and spiritually alive in Him. I speak and declare that my family are world changers and will impact nations for the glory of God. The Holy Spirit convicts and exposes the truth to us. I break all generational rebellion that would cause my family to resist the Holy Spirit in the name of Jesus (Acts 7:51). I break and release my children from all curses of rebellion and pride. I rebuke defiance, waywardness, indiscipline and bad behaviour. None of my family will reject the Word of the Lord (1 Sam. 15:23). We will not be proud or vain. I take authority and cast out every strongman of rebellion in my household in the name of Jesus. My children will love the Lord and keep His commandments (John 14:15). I claim all my children back to the Lord and set them free from any yoke of rebellion and witchcraft. This is my prayer and declaration in Jesus' name.

PRAY FOR CHILDREN OF THE WORLD:

Pray they are set free from the curse of rebellion and will not resist the Holy Spirit.

- WEEK 33 -

DECLARATIONS
FOR SANCTIFICATION

Sanctification is a calling; it is the will of God for our lives. It is a calling to align ourselves with God's will and cleanse ourselves from sin. It is the process of becoming more like Christ by purifying our hearts and minds through repentance and prayer. As parents and believers in Christ, our children are "holy", meaning they are "set apart" for the glory of God. That does not mean they are perfect or "sinless" because they are humans, but God calls them to be more like Jesus (to be separated and set apart from sin). This process of becoming more like Christ is called sanctification – to be different, set apart from those around us, and made holy. It is a call to put off the old self of sin and iniquity and put on the new man, one filled by the Spirit. It is our growth in grace to become more Christ-like. I pray that your children will live a life of holiness and grow in His grace. May God's Holy Spirit change us and our children's hearts in the name of Jesus.

Words of Wisdom: Jesus is the author of our sanctification. God did not call us to uncleanness, but in holiness (1 Thess. 4: 7). His grace sanctifies us. He chose us to be a people for His treasured possession, not because we are better than others, but because He loves us. The Lord set His love on our children and family. He commands that we live according to His Word and not return to our old sinful ways. For the Lord to work in and through our family, all we need is a sincere heart and desire to know him better.

Scripture Meditation: 1 Thessalonians 5: 23

"Now may the God of peace Himself sanctify you through and through [that is, separate you from profane and vulgar things, make you pure and whole and undamaged—consecrated to Him— set apart for His purpose]; and may your spirit and soul and body be kept complete and [be found] blameless at the coming of our Lord Jesus Christ."

Your Declaration: I declare that my family live a life of holiness, pleasing to the Lord. We have been made unto the Lord, wisdom, righteousness, sanctification and redemption. We live a sanctified life. We are sanctified through the truth of the Word. My children are sanctified completely by the God of peace Himself. Their whole spirit, soul and body are preserved blameless at the coming of our Lord Jesus Christ (1 Thess. 5:23). They repent and turn away from any sin in their lives. They are washed with the water of the Word. The Lord opens their spiritual eyes, to turn them from darkness to light, and from the power of Satan unto God, that they may receive forgiveness of sins, and an inheritance among those who have been sanctified by faith in Christ (Acts 26:18). The hand of the wicked will not drive my family away from the presence of God. We are covered with God's robe of righteousness and caused to be made blameless in His holy eyes by grace through faith. Our lives bring glory to God. We are available for God's purpose and separated from things profane. My children are delivered from living a life of ungodliness. They will be a vessel for honour, sanctified and useful for the Master, prepared for every good work (2 Tim. 2: 21). This is my prayer and declaration in Jesus' name.

PRAY FOR CHILDREN OF THE WORLD:

Pray that they live a life of holiness, pleasing to the Lord.

- WEEK 34 -

DECLARATIONS AGAINST IMMORALITY

We currently live in a time and place where a person is more likely to be confronted with the possibility of engaging in sexually tempting behaviour than they were at any other time or place in human history. Sexual immorality can be overtly immoral in its presentation and covertly sinful in its execution. The effects of a parent's sexual sin can be passed down through their family line and pollute subsequent generations of their descendants. As parents, we are well aware that our children will face the challenge of trying to overcome their sinful tendencies in this world, which is a reality for which we must prepare them. Sin exerts tremendous effort on them daily to secure a foothold, spread its roots, and ultimately gain control of our children so that it can triumph in its war against them. They are drawn in by many different things, such as movies, books, articles in magazines, and video games. Because of these things, it is easy for young people, regardless of whether they have undergone the experience of being born again, to give in to temptations, stray off course, and turn their backs on God. *"There is a way that seems right to a man and appears straight before him, but the end of that way is the way that leads to death" [Proverbs 16:25].*

God did not create sexual immorality, and anything that is not from God comes from the devil, the author of everything evil. Anything that originates from the devil is a lie and a fraud, and its end goal is destruction. The ways of the devil may appear attractive to man, but in the end, they will only lead to the individual's downfall. God's deepest desire is for our families to live lives free of sexual immorality, guided by the Holy Spirit. Your children will not fall prey to the enemy in Jesus name.

Words of Wisdom: Education, in addition to prayer, is one of the most effective weapons in the fight against sexual immorality. As guardians, we must launch a counteroffensive against the devious plots of the enemy. Fornication is a double-edged sword that slashes away at a person's soul, so we have a responsibility to educate our children that their bodies are holy in the eyes of the Lord. Let them know that sexual immorality is a sin that one commits against God as well as against their own body. Therefore, our children need to learn that they should avoid engaging in sexual misconduct. In Matthew 26:41, Jesus advised his followers to watch and pray in order to avoid giving in to temptation. *"Watch and pray, lest you enter into temptation. The spirit indeed is willing, but the flesh is weak."*

Scripture Meditation: 1 Thessalonians 4:3-7
"For this is the will of God, that you be sanctified [separated and set apart from sin]: that you abstain and back away from sexual immorality; that each of you know how to control his own body in holiness and honour [being available for God's purpose and separated from things profane], not [to be used] in lustful passion, like the Gentiles who do not know God and are ignorant of His will; and that [in this matter of sexual misconduct] no man shall transgress and defraud his brother because the Lord is the avenger in all these things, just as we have told you before and

solemnly warned you. For God has not called us to impurity, but to holiness [to be dedicated, and set apart by behaviour that pleases Him, whether in public or in private]."

Your Declaration: I declare that sin will have no power over my family in the name of Jesus (Rom. 6:14). We walk in the Spirit and shall not fulfil the lust of the flesh (Gal. 5:16). I bring the authority of Jesus Christ, His rule and dominion, and the complete work of Christ into my family and my home. I call upon the authority of the Lord Jesus Christ and the finished work of Christ to stand against every evil power that is advancing against my family. I plead the blood of Jesus Christ against every foul spirit of immorality, power and device of Satan, and I do so in the name of the Father, the Son, and the Holy Spirit. None of my family will be consumed by lustful thoughts. I release my children from the influence of any spirit of whoredom. I bind and cast out sexual perversion from among my children and from our home. I cast out and set all of my children and family free from the control of any spirit spouses, and I bind the curse of sexual immorality, lust, fornication and adultery. The devil will not enslave my family in the name of Jesus. I cast out all perverted spirits and sever all ties with demons based on sin, the flesh, or sacrifice. My children are delivered from the spirit of this world, the lust of the flesh, the lust of the eyes, and the pride of life. They will have no fellowship with demons, nor will they partake of the table of devils (1 Cor. 10:20-21). I bind and rebuke all spirits that cause lustful and fantastical thinking in my family. We do not have any affection for this world or the things that exist in it (1 John 2:15). We are victorious over the world as a result of the work of the Holy Spirit. We flee sexual immorality in any form, whether thought or behaviour, whether visual or written (1 Cor. 6:18). My children have been crucified with Christ. As a result, they refuse to allow sin to reign in their bodies and to obey the lust that sin brings (Rom. 6:6-12). They will not yield to temptation or lustful desires. Sin shall not have dominion over me or my family, for we are not under law (as slaves), but under unmerited grace (Rom. 6:14). This is my prayer and declaration in Jesus' name.

PRAY FOR CHILDREN OF THE WORLD:

Pray that sin shall not have dominion over them.

- WEEK 35 –

DECLARATIONS
FOR SEXUAL PURITY

Any breach of moral purity goes against God's good and perfect will for our children's lives. His stated will is that we abstain from sexual immorality. "For this is the will of God, that you be sanctified [separated and set apart from sin]: that you abstain and back away from sexual immorality" (1 Thess. 4:3 AMP). Therefore, God wants our children to be morally pure. "For this is the will of God, your sanctification; that is, that you abstain from sexual immorality."

Unfortunately, a whole generation of young people struggle with purity and feel guilty because they have failed repeatedly. Based on some statistics, 9 out of 10 teens say they would be more likely not to engage in sex if their parents would talk to them about it. As parents, we must push through the awkwardness and have those talks. We must discuss issues about sexuality, modesty, and body image with our children; otherwise, someone else will! It is not only by prayer alone; we need to talk. For example, about scenarios they might encounter whilst out with friends that could lead to sexual temptation, such as being out too late at night, drinking alcohol, and spending too much time together alone. Ask them to think about the consequences of their particular actions and potential exit strategies if they find themselves in an uncomfortable situation. After discussion, pray with them and reassure them of the love of God.

Contrary to popular belief, young people want to hear what adults have to say. While it may be uncomfortable to discuss sex with your child, they will learn about it from friends or on the Internet if you do not speak with them. Our children can't change the past, but we can do something about the future. Then, by God's grace, they can be clean and pure by the power in the name of Jesus.

Words of Wisdom: God has, out of His love for us, given the command of reserving sex for marriage to protect us, not stifle us. Our children need this protection. Talk about sexual purity with your teen, and encourage them to flee from sexual immorality (1 Cor. 6:18). Pray with your children, and let them know that any form of sexual sin will hurt God's name, hurt them and hurt others. His clearly stated will is that we abstain from sexual immorality. A practical tool for encouraging your child toward a life of sexual purity is, for example, getting their calendar busy. Get them engaged in team sports, develop their gifts and talents, and use their youthful energy to benefit others through community service. Get them engaged in a church youth group, drama team, involvement in the choir, ushering, hospitality etc. Also, involvement in after-school clubs and activities means less time to hook up and more time for positive social and emotional development. By doing this, and with prayer support, they are removing themselves from the troubles that too much isolation can create.

Scripture Meditation: 1 Corinthians 6:18-20 (AMP)
"Run away from sexual immorality [in any form, whether thought

or behaviour, whether visual or written]. Every other sin that a man commits is outside the body, but the one who is sexually immoral sins against his own body. Do you not know that your body is a temple of the Holy Spirit who is within you, whom you have [received as a gift] from God, and that you are not your own [property]? You were bought with a price [you were actually purchased with the precious blood of Jesus and made His own]. So then, honour and glorify God with your body."

Your Declaration: I declare that my children keep their hearts with all diligence, for out of it springs the issues of life (Prov. 4:23). Their body is a living sacrifice, holy and pleasing to God (Romans 12:1). They run from sexual sin, fornication and adultery. The Lord gives them the grace to live a sexually pure life. Sin cannot enslave my children in the name of Jesus. Christ has overcome their sins and weaknesses. My children belong to God and have overcome the world. He who is in them is greater than he who is in the world (1 John 4:4). Their body is God's temple, and everything detestable is gone. They choose to be pure because they love God and want to follow His plan for their life. I take authority and break the power of Satan over their sexual struggles in the name of Jesus. Through the power, majesty and authority in the name of Jesus, I cut, sever, break, and burn all cords, snares, controls, and bondage used by the evil spirits of Jezebel and Ahab over my children. Each of my children belongs to Jesus Christ, the Son of God, Almighty, Everlasting, King of Kings, and Lord of lords! God chose them in Christ before the foundation of the world to be holy and blameless before the Father (Eph. 1:4). They are sanctified, separated and set apart from sin. They abstain from sexual immorality and live a sexually pure life (1 Thess. 4:3). This is my prayer and declaration in Jesus' name.

PRAY FOR CHILDREN OF THE WORLD:

That they are sanctified, separated and set apart from sin.

- WEEK 36 -

DECLARATIONS
AT UNIVERSITY/COLLEGE

As our children head off to university, there is a world of unknowns to explore. When we drop them off at university, we release them to a world we can't control. They have a pool of potential new friends, money deposited in their bank account, total freedom from home and countless opportunities for adventure. For others, it might be a scary time, like a nightmare with fear of the unknown, which brings anxieties and worries. They are finally solely responsible for their own lives! We need to be praying for our youth! Prayer is our first opportunity to fight for them and their destiny. As they leave the comfort of home and head off to university, we pray they will adapt well to their new surroundings and that God will surround them with genuine and wise friends who will challenge them to walk more closely with Him. Let us pray that God will lead our children to a good local church where they can serve Him at university. A new church family where they can be loved and looked out for whilst growing in the love of God.

Success is hard work, perseverance, diligence, learning, studying and sacrifice. University is a place of learning. I pray that your children will excel and love learning more deeply and widely in their chosen degrees; they will work hard and focus on their studies. They will not only work hard and earn their degree but also grow closer to the Lord as they advance in their walk with Christ. I pray God will give them wisdom in their choices on what to do and what not to do and have peace.

Words of Wisdom: As your children go through university/college, they must cling to the Word of God. Although worry, anxiety and thoughts of failure can infiltrate their minds and drag them down, as long as you diligently pray for them and commit their care to the Lord, He will take care of the rest. God did not bring your children unto this earth to abandon them; He stays by their side to guide and empower them through good and bad times.

Scripture Meditation: John 14:27 (AMP)

"Peace I leave with you; My [perfect] peace I give to you; not as the world gives do I give to you. Do not let your heart be troubled, nor let it be afraid. [Let My perfect peace calm you in every circumstance and give you courage and strength for every challenge.]"

Your Declaration: I declare that my children are faithful to the academic calling that God has placed on their lives. Their university/college is blessed. They will attend their lectures and complete all their assignments and modules. They have a retentive memory, keen understanding and the ability to grasp things correctly and fundamentally. They become all that God desires them to be. They fit in with other students and interact with lecturers. They will complete their modules and assignments within the specified time. They will not be distracted but have great enthusiasm for their studies. Each lecture, seminar, and class brings fresh inspiration to their studies. They find peace and rest in the shadow of the Almighty (Ps. 91:1). God meets all their physical, mental and spiritual needs according to the riches of His glory in Christ Jesus (Phil. 4:19). Evil shall not befall them, nor shall any plague come near their university/college, or accommodation in the name of Jesus (Ps. 91:10). They will not follow the voice of the evil one or join bad groups. The enemy shall not outwit them, nor the son of wickedness afflict them. The enemy will not defeat them, nor will the evil one overpower them. The Lord will steady them with His hand and strengthen them with His powerful arm (Ps. 89: 21-22). They will not fail their current academic year. They will get promoted to the next academic year in the name of Jesus. I cover their university/college and accommodation with the blood of Jesus. They win favour in the sight of their lecturers, university/college administration, and fellow students. This is my prayer and declaration in Jesus' name.

PRAY FOR CHILDREN OF THE WORLD:

Pray they will not follow the voice of the evil one or join bad groups at university/college.

DECLARATIONS
AT SCHOOL

Being a good student honours God and gives Him glory. Our children have been through a lot in recent years with the pandemic, so it's understandable if they find school difficult. They must do their best at school for the glory of God, but school can be challenging for children, and they might find everyday tasks like getting ready in the morning more difficult. They might also feel anxious about current events, worrying and thinking about what might happen. They might not feel as confident in their schoolwork, or feel less motivated to do school or homework. Their marks might drop because they find it very difficult to focus in class and might not want to go to school or even refuse. In some rare cases, some might be truant without their parents knowing, but things can get better with prayer, supplication and thanksgiving.

Never stop praying for your children. God takes care of them when you are not with them. He is a good God! I encourage you to hand over your children's education, school, and friends to God. Surrender the school, all teachers and staff to Jesus. Pray over the school and plead the blood of Jesus on teachers and fellow students. Pray over the atmosphere in the classrooms, lecture theatres and plead the blood of Jesus against demonic activities and assignments of the enemy. Pray the Spirit of God will take charge over the school, that His Spirit of peace will rule and reign.

The Bible tells us that instead of being anxious about anything, we should pray and give thanks to Him! In the place of prayer, we see things shift in our children's lives. When we pray for them, God intervenes and meets them at their point of need.

Words of Wisdom: The Lord will help your children achieve success in their education. Show them scriptures they can use to pray before leaving for school or college. Teach them to pray for their teachers and fellow students. The Lord will continue to guard and guide your children in their academic journey. He is a faithful God.

Scripture Meditation: Isaiah 26:3-4

"You will keep in perfect and constant peace the one whose mind is steadfast [that is, committed and focused on You—in both inclination and character], because he trusts and takes refuge in You [with hope and confident expectation]. "Trust [confidently] in the Lord forever [He is your fortress, your shield, your banner], for the Lord God is an everlasting Rock [the Rock of Ages]."

Your Declaration: I declare that my children are motivated, focused and disciplined at school. They are faithful to the academic calling that God has placed on their lives. Whatever they do at school, they will work at it with all their heart (Col. 3:23). They are focused and organised in their academic studies. They have more understanding than all their teachers (Ps. 119:99). They don't do the bare minimum in academics; they go above and beyond their teacher's expectations. They work hard, put in the effort and pay attention in class. They are proactive and intentional, and all their school work is excellent. They complete their homework and submit it within the specified time. They will not grow tired or weary in their studies and will not stumble and fall. The Lord teaches all my children, and great shall be their peace (Ps. 54:13). They understand more than the ancients (Ps. 119:100). Impossibility is not an option. They can do all things through Christ who strengthens and empowers them (Phil. 4:13). They will not follow the enemy's voice and join bad groups or gangs. I rebuke and bind bullying and intimidation. They shall not hear the voice of a stranger. Their ways at school are ways of pleasantness, and all their paths are peace (Prov. 3:17). I bind all distractions assigned against their academic life and progress in the name of Jesus. The Lord promotes my children at every educational level. He is their confidence and will keep their foot from being caught at school (Prov. 3:26). They have a retentive memory and quick understanding. They win favour in God's sight and with their teachers, lecturers, administration, and fellow students. This is my prayer and declaration in Jesus' name.

PRAY FOR CHILDREN OF THE WORLD:

Pray they will not grow tired or weary in their education and will not stumble and fall out of school.

- WEEK 38 –

DECLARATIONS AGAINST BONDAGE TO DRUGS & ALCOHOLISM

Bondage has been a struggle for humanity since the beginning of our story in the Garden of Eden, and God's children are no exception. God warns us against harmful behaviours such as binge drinking and drug use. He knows these activities will destroy our body, mind, and soul, drawing our family away from Him and toward earthly ruin and eternal death. I pray this evil spirit of bondage and enslavement will not visit our homes in the name of Jesus. Children of today, regardless of age or the ethnicity of their parents, are raised in a society where it is easy to obtain drugs and alcohol. Parents who engage in harmful behaviours with substances like alcohol and drugs also impact how their children understand and view the use of those substances. Likewise, parents who misuse alcohol and drugs also influence how their children perceive and understand the use of alcohol and drugs.

Addiction is when we let something take control of us and become our master, which makes us bound to it. Any addiction is a form of idolatry, whether to alcohol, drugs, prescribed medication, pornography, cigarettes, or even food. The first written commandment in the Bible is, "You shall not have any other gods before Me", which is extremely important. Christ came to set us free from enslavement resulting from our sins, including addiction. "He has sent Me (Jesus) to preach good news to the poor, heal those whose hearts have been broken, announce freedom to all captives, and pardon all prisoners," (Isaiah 61:1). The second commandment in Exodus 20 states that you are not to prostrate yourself before them or serve them. When someone is addicted to something, they essentially worship that addiction as if it were their God and submit to it. It is a form of sin known as idolatry. They are forced into servitude and become a slave to it. Jesus said, "Everyone who sins is a slave to sin" (John 8:34).

Many people, both young and old, are passing away gradually due to the grip that addiction has on them. They are bound. The power of Jesus Christ is the only thing that breaks this bondage. Jesus came to heal the broken-hearted, proclaim liberty to the captives, and open the prison doors to those who are bound. He also came to open the eyes of those who are blind (Isaiah 61:1). *"Therefore, if the Son sets you free, you will indeed be free" (John 8:36).*

Words of Wisdom: When the Holy Spirit reigns supreme in our children's hearts, they can experience the power, guidance, and knowledge of forgiveness, peace, and hope that comes from God. He will assist in the healing of any addiction and break any bondage that may exist within the family. The Holy Bible is the ideal model for how we should live our lives and think, feel, and behave. When our children are guided and filled with the Holy Spirit, they can feel secure knowing they are loved, connected, and a part of God. When our youth turn away from God and attempt to replace Him with other things, they make poor decisions, get into arguments with the people they care about and turn to substances like alcohol to feel better about themselves. Let us pray the Holy Spirit will reign supreme in the hearts of our children.

Scripture Meditation: Romans 6:16-19 (AMP)

"Do you not know that when you continually offer yourselves to someone to do his will, you are the slaves of the one whom you obey, either [slaves] of sin, which leads to death, or of obedience, which leads to righteousness (right standing with God)? But thank God that though you were slaves of sin, you became obedient with all your heart to the standard of teaching in which you were instructed and to which you were committed. And having been set free from sin, you have become the slaves of righteousness [of conformity to God's will and purpose]. I am speaking in [familiar] human terms because of your natural limitations [your spiritual immaturity]. For just as you presented your bodily members as slaves to impurity and to [moral] lawlessness, leading to further lawlessness, so now offer your members [your abilities, your talents] as slaves to righteousness, leading to sanctification [that is, being set apart for God's purpose]."

Your Declaration: I declare that every yoke of bondage is completely destroyed in my family (Gal 5:1). The Lord protects my family from intoxication, alcoholism, and perversion. It will not dominate our lives. My children will not become intoxicated on wine, which is a form of dissipation. Instead, they are filled with the Holy Spirit (Eph 5:18). They are not swayed by alcoholic beverages such as wine and beer or other chemicals that alter their state of mind. They are not in any way dependent on alcohol or illegal substances. They are not bound to anyone or anything in any way. My children behave in a decent and honourable manner as if in broad daylight, refraining from carousing and intoxication, sexual promiscuity and irresponsibility, and quarrelling and jealousy. But they wrap themselves with the Lord Jesus Christ and neither provide for nor even consider satisfying the flesh's inappropriate wants. They are selective about the company they keep and the people they associate with. They will not associate with someone who claims to be a brother but is sexually immoral or selfish, an idolater or a slanderer, an alcoholic or a con-artist. They are selective in the people they let into their lives. The direction of their life is positive. They will not fall into the trap of the devil, which would lead them to succumb to temptation. Their hearts are not weighed down by the intoxication and concerns of this life. They prioritise living for the Lord and are saved from the wicked. The spirit of Belial does not operate in their lives. The adversary will not devour them. They put on the breastplate of faith and love, and as a helmet the hope of salvation (1 Thess. 5:8). I plead the blood of Jesus on my family and command all powers of darkness to flee! This is my prayer and declaration in Jesus' name.

PRAY FOR CHILDREN OF THE WORLD:

That their lives are pointed in the right direction, and they are not caught in the devil's snare to cause them to fall into temptation.

DECLARATIONS AGAINST LAZINESS / LACK OF MOTIVATION

Everyone struggles with motivation at some point. Our children and teenagers are no exceptions. Perhaps your child is not motivated! He/she seems to have no drive, backbone, and desire to do much more than play video games and watch TV all day. They do not complete their homework or assignments. You might ask yourself, "Why doesn't this child focus more on his/her studies?" Like you, many parents believe they have a "lazy child". The main issue is a lack of motivation. God's Word makes it abundantly plain that we are to work hard and give our best effort. *"Whatever you do, do it heartily, as to the Lord and not to men" (Col. 3:23).* I pray your children will grow up to be successful, self-motivated, hardworking adults.

Words of Wisdom: Never lose hope that your child will change; always believe. Declare, pronounce, and prophesy the outcome you want to see. Pray and speak aloud into the atmosphere of their bedroom. Keep declaring these prayers, and you will witness God's power at work in your children's lives. Prayer does change things!

Scripture Meditation: Proverbs 10:5 (AMP)
"He who gathers during summer and takes advantage of his opportunities is a son who acts wisely, but he who sleeps during

harvest and ignores the moment of opportunity is a son who acts shamefully."

Your Declaration: I declare that whatever my children's hand finds to do, they do it with all their might (Eccl. 9: 10). They will not sit around all day doing nothing. They get up and get going in the name of Jesus. They take a step forward in completing their goals and do what needs to be done when it needs to be done. Procrastination is a destroyer of blessings. It will not destroy my children's life and blessings in the name of Jesus. My family are productive and bears much fruit. I rebuke the power and activity of laziness in my children's life. Spirit of procrastination, I command you to flee from my children's minds, thoughts, bodies, mouths and entire lives this day and forever. They are set free from a mindset of procrastination and sloth. I rebuke excess sleeping and useless discussions in group chats and social media, stealing their time. I cast out any demon of slumber from their lives and break the spirit of laziness and procrastination holding my children down. They do not do what the old nature wants. They run their lives by the Spirit of God since they have life through the Spirit. Their lives are ordered day by day by the Holy Spirit. None of my family is lazy. This is my prayer and declaration in Jesus' name.

PRAY FOR CHILDREN OF THE WORLD:
Pray they will not sit around doing nothing all day.

DECLARATIONS AGAINST LYING & DECEPTION

The Bible mentions seven things that are an abomination to God in Proverbs 6:16-19, two of which include lying: "a lying tongue" and "a false witness who speaks lies." God despises a deceitful tongue! There is no truth in a lie. "I have not written to you because you do not know the truth, but because you do know it, and because no lie [nothing false, no deception] is of the truth" (1 John 2:21). Lying is the deliberate telling of falsehood to mislead or induce someone to believe an inaccuracy. How often has your child been caught lying? It could be because they want to avoid punishment or are frightened of upsetting you if they reveal the truth. Unfortunately, children can be deceptive at times. In Acts 5:1-9, Ananias and Sapphira sold land and retained some money for themselves, but they lied to the Apostles and said they had given the full price for the land. Peter asked, "Ananias, why has Satan filled your heart to lie to the Holy Spirit and keep back part of the price of the land for yourself?... Why have you conceived this thing in your heart? You have not lied to men but to God." They had lied to God!

Exodus 8:28–29 explains how Pharaoh tricked Moses into believing he would release the Israelites from slavery if God stopped the plagues. However, Pharaoh broke his promise when God did what Pharaoh had asked. In 2 Corinthians 11:13-15, "False apostles" are called "deceitful workers" because they pretend to be servants of Christ, angels of light, transforming themselves into ministers of righteousness. Numerous pastors position themselves as men of God who teach His word, but they teach doctrines not found in the Bible. God hates lying mouths because they bring him dishonour.

But what about our children? Are they guilty of telling lies? We must pray that our children will not grow up to be liars and deceivers and that they will do everything to the glory of God. To avoid dishonesty and lying, we need to be aware of the factors that lead to our children's wrongdoing. Every deception has roots in the human heart and Satan's corrupting influence. In John 8:44, Jesus said regarding Satan: "There is no truth in him. When he speaks a lie, he speaks from his own resources, for he is a liar and the father of it." Satan encourages men to lie. When our children utter lies, they act under Satan's influence, yet the root of the problem resides within each of their hearts. If we want to see a change in our children, we first need to pray that God will transform the way they think and ask Him to renew their hearts through the authority of His Word. I pray that God will fill the heart and souls of your children with the truth of His Word in Jesus' name.

Words of Wisdom: The truth is that our children have all been guilty of telling lies at one time or another. If we want them to enjoy spiritual communion with God, we must pray that they will love the truth, that we will teach them to speak the truth, and that God will remove lying and deception from their lives. Parents, please take heed not to lie to your children. A child is more likely to lie if they are raised by a habitually dishonest parent. When parents tell their children lies, they are modelling that lying is, in fact, acceptable.

Scripture Meditation: James 5:12 (AMP)

"But above all, my fellow believers, do not swear, either by heaven or by earth or with any other oath; but let your yes be [a truthful] yes, and your no be [a truthful] no, so that you may not fall under judgment."

Your Declaration: I declare that my family stay far away from deception, corruption, and lying tongues. The deceiver will not release deception into our hearts in the name of Jesus. I bind and rebuke the angel of light (2 Cor. 11:14). My children will not heed deceiving spirits and demons' doctrines. They will not speak lies, and their conscience will not be seared (1 Tim. 4:1). No man will deceive them in the name of Jesus (Matt. 24:4). The enemy will not persuade my children to believe lies disguised as the truth or things that sound good or right but are contrary to God's Word. I bind every falsehood, every deception, and every word of false prophecy that has been unleashed into my family, and I declare that it will not come to pass in the name of Jesus. I command that every veil be removed from my children's eyes in the name of Jesus. I destroy every stronghold that the enemy has built around my children's minds and cast down every high thing that exalts itself against the knowledge of Christ. I command it to crash to the ground in the name of Jesus! My children have the mind of Christ, and I bring every one of their thoughts into captivity to the obedience of Christ (2 Cor. 10:5). They will not be dishonest. They speak the truth and stand by the truth. Their conscience is not weak and will not be defiled by the enemy (1 Cor. 8:7). They are free from the spirit of lies. I speak Psalm 141: 3-4 over my family,

"Set a guard, O Lord, over our mouths; keep watch over the door of our lips [to keep us from speaking thoughtlessly]. We will not incline our hearts to [consent to or tolerate] any evil thing or to practice deeds of wickedness with people who plan and do evil, and let us not eat of their delicacies (be tempted by their gain). I now proclaim that as of this day forward, my children are severed from all foundations constructed on lies. I condemn every lie and break the power and stronghold of deception in the hearts of my family. This is my prayer and declaration in Jesus' name.

If you suspect your child of lying, pray with him/her to repent of the sin of lying, and ask God to forgive him/her.

Lead them in the following prayer:

Father God, I, _____ ask your forgiveness for the sin of lying. I repent and ask you to reveal why I lie so much. Please forgive me for lying to my family, trying to please others and getting away with things. Jesus, I ask that you break and destroy the stronghold of lying in me. The Bible says Satan is a liar and the Father of lies, and I don't want to speak his language. I want to speak your Word, Lord, the language of truth and righteousness. Therefore, I rebuke Satan and cast the spirit of lying out of my life. I command you lying spirit to leave me now and never come back in the name of Jesus. I reject all your lies in the name of Jesus. I ask you, heavenly Father, to fill me with your Holy Spirit, fill me with your truth, and fill the rest of my family with your truth. Fill me with all the fullness of God and deliver me from any compulsion to lie from now and forever in Jesus name, I pray. Amen.

PRAY FOR CHILDREN OF THE WORLD:

Pray that the Lord will break down every stronghold the enemy has built around their minds and cast down arguments and every high thing that exalts itself against the knowledge of God.

- WEEK 41 -

DECLARATIONS
AGAINST BULLYING & HARASSMENT

Bullies are individuals who tease and harass others to bring them down. They get a sick thrill from causing other people pain and misery. They do not value kindness but rather prefer to engage in hostile behaviour. I have had to pray and ask God for help defending myself and my family from bullies. I've been through the pain and understand how it feels.

The experience of being bullied at work, school, college, or university is comparable to entering a lion's den. In the book of Daniel, we learn how God saved Daniel from certain death by rescuing him from the lion's mouth. God intervened and silenced the lions' roars. The Lord will end the roaring of the lions who are bullying your family in the name of Jesus!

"Then Daniel said to the king, 'O king, live forever! My God sent his angel and shut the lions' mouths, and they have not harmed me, because I was found blameless before him; and also before you, O king, I have done no harm" (Daniel 6:21-22)

I don't think it is too much to ask God to shut the lions' mouths (bullies), as we send our children into the den (world) every day. So I encourage you to make this a daily exercise by praying that God will shut the mouth of the lions as you drive your children to school, college, or university. Another prayer against bullies is the

Prayer of Jehoshaphat. In 2 Chronicles 20, Israel's enemies have banded together to destroy the people of Israel. The sheer size of the military might must have frightened King Jehoshaphat. He was so terrified that he resolved to seek God and summoned the people of God to fast and seek God alongside himself (2 Chronicles 20:1-4). Other nations are bullying his nation. This is the specific distress he is experiencing. So Jehoshaphat stands in the courtyard of the temple in Jerusalem and publicly prays to God for assistance (2 Chronicles 20:5).

In the case of Jehoshaphat, God turned the bullies against each other (2 Chronicles 20:22-23). The Lord will rescue your family from the hands of those who mistreat you in the name of Jesus.

Words of Wisdom: If your child is being bullied at school, college, university or even in the office, you must identify the perpetrator. Mention their name in prayer at the altar, bringing them before God. Raise your hands in prayer and inform God that your child is being bullied. When a child is bullied, we need assistance in fighting back. Pray to God and tell Him you cannot fight bullies without His help. Ask Him to fight the battle for you. Look to Him for help, and then wait for the answer. God will answer your prayers. In Jehoshaphat's case, God did answer the prayer. His response was clear: "The battle is not yours, but Mine. Trust me!" (2 Chronicles 20:15).

Scripture Meditation: *Deuteronomy 31:6 (AMP)*
"Be strong and courageous, do not be afraid or tremble in dread before them, for it is the Lord your God who goes with you. He will not fail you or abandon you."

Psalm 9:9-10 (AMP) - *"The Lord is a refuge for the oppressed, a stronghold in times of trouble."*

Your Declaration: I declare that the Lord protects my family from the dangers of the enemy (bullies). They will not be harassed or mistreated in any way. He hides them from the secret plots of the wicked (Ps. 64:1-2). They will not be afraid of bullies because He is their light and salvation. Whenever the children are afraid, they will trust the Lord (Ps. 56:3). The Lord rescues them from emotional and physical abuse. I bind and cast out all demons of fear and timidity in the name of Jesus (2 Tim. 1:7). I destroy all demonic attacks and command all bullies to leave my children in the name of Jesus! Words of scorn and discouragement will not prosper in my children's lives. All those who utter insults at them will themselves suffer the effects of their wrongdoing in the name of Jesus. I declare that God will cause the evil people who go around bullying children to fail in their actions. The Lord's Angels will protect my children from bullies wherever they go. In the name of Jesus, I bind, rebuke, and cast out any demonic, harassing, bullying spirit assigned against my children and family. I declare that the blood of Jesus Christ has broken your powers, and I command you not to touch or intimidate my family in any way. The Lord has brought my children out of a horrible pit, out of the miry clay, and set their feet upon a rock, and established their steps (Ps. 40:2). He has put a new song in their mouth from this day forward and forever. This is my prayer and declaration in Jesus' name.

PRAY FOR CHILDREN OF THE WORLD:

Pray that the Lord will keep and protect all children of the world from bullying and harassment.

DECLARATIONS
AGAINST SUDDEN DEATH & SUICIDE

Suicidal thoughts and depression can make people feel isolated. Changes in normal behaviour, such as trouble sleeping or eating, and being very quiet and alone for extended periods, are some indications of depression and suicide risk. Your child may be having a bad day, but if this mood has been going on for weeks or months, it could be a sign of something more serious. How will you know if your child is thinking about suicide? According to research, in families devastated by the suicide of a child, poor communication between parents and children is one of the most typical characteristics of those households. When a youngster is contemplating suicide, there are usually three or more concerns or circumstances at play in his or her life at the time. For example, parents could be going through a divorce, which might warrant having to move home, start a new school, make new friends, and other emotional factors around the home for which the child may try to hide their unhappiness. They're often too embarrassed to reveal their sadness to others, including mum and dad. Boys, in particular, try to hide their emotions in the misguided belief that displaying their feelings is a sign of weakness. When your child starts dropping comments like, "Everyone would be better off without me", "I wish I could sleep and never wake up.", "Nothing matters", "I have let you down." Don't mock or yell at them; instead, be willing to be non-judgmental and listen to what he or she is saying, which is: "I need your love and attention because I'm in a lot of pain, and I can't seem to stop it on my own." The immediate focus must be on consoling and comforting your child, speaking to them in a calm and understanding voice.

Let's not wait for our children to come to us with their problems or concerns. I would advise that you knock on the door, sit gently on the bed, and say, "You seem sad and unhappy. Would you like to talk? Maybe I can help. How are you feeling?" Even if your child is not communicating, it is vital to listen, sit quietly with them and spend some time together. Encourage your youngster not to withdraw from family and friends. Even if they aren't saying anything, hug them nevertheless. Your presence can make a difference. I recommend that you assist your child in receiving counselling, prayer support, and other forms of treatment that will assist in making things better.

Words of Wisdom: Your child needs to know that they are not alone and that everyone, even parents experience feelings of sadness, depression, or anxiety from time to time. Without diminishing their pain, reassure them that these difficult times will not persist indefinitely. Strengthen yourself with proclamations and God's promises to help your family combat negative thoughts. Get prophetic words and favourite Bible verses together and speak them out loud over your family. There is hope for your children. Experts advise 30 to 40 minutes of exercise per day, two to five times per week. Any exercise will suffice; it is essential that children and adolescents enjoy the activity and continue to participate on a consistent basis, which should help keep their minds active and occupied in a healthy way.

Scripture Meditation: Romans 8:1-2 (AMP)

"Therefore there is now no condemnation [no guilty verdict, no punishment] for those who are in Christ Jesus [who believe in Him as personal Lord and Saviour]. For the law of the Spirit of life [which is] in Christ Jesus [the law of our new being] has set you free from the law of sin and of death."

Your Declaration: I declare that my family have life, and we are not appointed unto death (Ps 102:20). The law of the Spirit of Life in Christ Jesus has delivered us from the power of sin and death (Romans 8:2). No evil shall touch any member of my family in the name of Jesus (Job 5:19). We shall not die prematurely. We are delivered from sudden death and destruction (Ps 107:20). The Lord will not allow the destroyer to strike my children (Exod. 12:23). I bind every demonic plot of suicide and silence the voice of death. My children's souls are delivered from death, their eyes from tears, and their feet from falling (Ps 116:8). I break and release my family from all curses of death and destruction in the name of Jesus. The eye of the Lord delivers our souls from death and keeps us alive in famine (Ps. 33:18-19). None of my family shall die before their time, but we shall all live and declare the works of the Lord (Ps. 118:17). I plead the blood of Jesus against the spirit of death and suicide. I command all spirits of depression, mania and insanity to loose my children in the name of Jesus. I break the curse of witchcraft and all mind control. Our God is the God of salvation and to Him belong escapes from death (Ps. 68:20). I am convinced that neither death, nor life, nor angels, nor principalities, nor things present and threatening, nor things to come, nor powers, nor height, nor depth, nor any other created thing will be able to separate my family from the love of

God, which is in Christ Jesus our Lord. (Rom. 8:38-39). In quietness and confidence shall be our strength (Isa. 30:15). God has come to give my children not just life, but abundant life (John 10:10), and all of His promises over their lives are "Yes and Amen!" (2 Corinthians 1:20). This is my prayer and declaration in Jesus' name.

PRAY FOR CHILDREN OF THE WORLD:
Pray that their souls are delivered from death and their feet from falling.

- WEEK 43 –

DECLARATIONS
FOR GOOD FRIENDSHIPS

Friendship is one of the greatest gifts in life. Our friends remain a hugely important part of our lives from childhood to adulthood. God has not put our children on earth with the intent for them to walk in solitude. Instead, he created them for relationships, and friendship is one of the most critical connections we make with others. Compassionate, God-fearing and kind friends are the people who get us through rough times. They often come to us with love and compassion, standing with us in prayer and walking through the valleys of life with us, speaking the right words of encouragement and helping us find strength in difficult times. In the Bible, 1 Samuel 18 tells us about the vital relationship between David and Jonathan, King Saul's son. They became the best of friends, and the Bible mentions that the soul of Jonathan was knit to the soul of David, and Jonathan loved him as himself (1 Sam. 18:1). David had just defeated Goliath and was brought before the king. Scripture says, "After David had finished talking with Saul, Jonathan became one in spirit with David, and he loved him as himself. From that day Saul kept David with him and did not let him return home to his family. And Jonathan made a covenant with David because he loved him as himself. Jonathan took off the robe he was wearing and gave it to David, along with his tunic, and even his sword, his bow and his belt." (1 Samuel 18:1–4).

After defeating Goliath, Jonathan recognises David's potential and offers David his robe, armour, sword, bow, and belt. He made a symbolic gesture of not only welcoming David into the family but also placing him ahead of himself in succession to the throne. Moreover, Jonathan displayed true friendship toward David. "He loved him as himself." Let us pray that the Lord will make way for healthy and godly relationships like the one of David and Jonathan to come into our children's lives.

The friendship principle here is that a good friend recognises the strengths and abilities of the other, and they are not afraid to promote one another above themselves. I pray God would lead godly friends and influences into your children's lives in the name of Jesus.

Words of Wisdom: Friendship is an essential part of life. From our children's earliest moments, friends profoundly impact their attitudes and behaviour. It is a vital part of their growing up and an essential part of their development. Your children's friendships have more power than you may realise, so I encourage you to pray that they choose their friends wisely and pray unhealthy friendships out of their lives. Above all, I pray your children will be a friend of God and be obedient to His will in the name of Jesus.

Scripture Meditation: Proverbs 17:17
"A friend loves at all times, And a brother is born for adversity."

John 15:12-15: "This is My commandment, that you love one another as I have loved you. Greater love has no one than this, than to lay down one's life for his friends. You are My friends if you do whatever I command you. No longer do I call you servants, for a servant does not know what his master is doing; but I have called you friends, for all things that I heard from My Father I have made known to you."

Your Declaration: I declare faithful and godly friends are added unto my children. They are blessed with genuine, trustworthy, steadfast and godly friends because their hearts are set upon God, and He sets His love upon them. Any relationship that would sabotage my family's destiny is broken in the name of Jesus. We have no interest in pursuing friendships that could harm our lives, reputation, or faith. We make wise choices in our friendships. We will not fall prey or be deceived by the enemy. The enemy shall not outwit us, nor the son of wickedness afflict or humiliate us (Ps. 89:22). My children attract friends who love the Lord and obey Him. They are not a companion of fools. They walk as companions with wise men, and they will be wise (Prov. 13:20). They will not experience harm nor be troubled or bullied by friends. They will not make friends with a hot-tempered man nor associate with one easily angered (Prov. 22:24). They choose their friends carefully, for the way of the wicked will not lead them astray (Prov. 12:26). They are truthful in their friendships/relationships, loyal, and find honour before the Lord. I bind and break any transfer of demonic spirits into my family by friends or associates of my children in the name of Jesus. With the Word of God, the sword of the Holy Spirit, I sever all evil soul ties between hostile persons and my children, and I plead the blood of Jesus over their minds, emotions and will, preventing these soul ties from ever being established in their lives. I break the power of evil friendships and cast out all spirits of witchcraft control and possessiveness by friends and family. This is my prayer and declaration in Jesus' name.

PRAY FOR CHILDREN OF THE WORLD:

Pray that they will not fall prey to the enemy, the enemy shall not outwit them, nor the wicked afflict or humiliate them.

DECLARATIONS
FOR FUTURE SPOUSE

Our children's most important decision is who they choose as their spouse. Praying for your child's future spouse is a powerful thing. It's essential to set aside time to pray. We must never underestimate the power of a praying parent that can reach far into future generations. Our desire and prayers are for our children to have a God-centred marriage. Marriage is a covenant that is binding until death, so it's crucial we must begin our intercessory prayers for future sons or daughters-in-law as soon as possible. God has a purpose for your children and their future marriage. It's never too late or too early to petition God on your child's behalf in all areas of life, especially concerning lifelong commitments. I pray God will direct your children towards a path that leads them to a lifelong companion who loves Jesus, who has their best interest in mind and can offer stability, love and support in a constantly unstable, changing and chaotic world.

Words of Wisdom: God knows who will complement your son/daughter and precisely who they will help complement. Spend some regular time in prayer to thank God for their future spouse, the gift of marriage, and the relational intimacy your son/daughter will experience through it. Ask God to lead them to the right decisions and pray that your children will wait patiently and faithfully for their future spouse until they cross paths.

Scripture Meditation: Matthew 7:7-8 (AMP)

"Ask and keep on asking and it will be given to you; seek and keep on seeking and you will find; knock and keep on knocking and the door will be opened to you. For everyone who keeps on asking receives, and he who keeps on seeking finds, and to him who keeps on knocking, it will be opened."

Your Declaration (For Son's Future Wife): I declare that my son's future wife seeks Christ and His Kingdom first (Matt. 6:33). She desires to be in the Word daily and strives to live a life that pleases the Lord. Christ is at the forefront of her everyday life. Her lamp does not go out by night (Prov. 31:18). The Lord grants her the spirit of wisdom and revelation in the knowledge of Him and opens the eyes of her understanding so that she knows the hope of God's calling (Eph. 1:17). She will not want to hurt my son because she will not want to hurt God, and does him good and not evil all the days of her life (Prov. 31:12). She will honour my son because she honours God. She is the right woman that God has in mind for him. My son will not marry a Jezebel or Delilah in the name of Jesus. The Lord reveals a godly wife to him. She speaks with wisdom, and on her tongue is the law of kindness (Prov. 31:26). She reflects the love of God and places her life in God's hands. The Lord draws her one step closer to Himself each day. She will choose to let the struggles of life make her better and not bitter. Strength and honour are her clothing (Prov. 31:25). Her love for my son flows from the abundance of a Spirit-filled heart. They will marry at the time God has set for them to marry. She completes her husband and loves him with Christlike love. This is my prayer and declaration in Jesus' name.

Declaration (For Daughter's Future Husband): I declare that above everything else, my daughter's future husband seeks Christ and His Kingdom first (Matt. 6:33). He desires to be in the Word daily and strives to live a life that pleases the Lord. He is loyal and kind, a man after God's own heart. He keeps God at the forefront of his everyday life. The Lord grants him the spirit of wisdom and revelation in the knowledge of Him. He is a Godly man who knows how to love the Lord and others with sincerity. He will not want to hurt my daughter because he will not want to hurt God. He will honour my daughter because he honours God. He is the man that God has in mind for her. He meets my daughter's needs and loves her with Christlike love—a godly servant leader of their home. He is a man of the Word, a doer of the Word and not just a hearer (James 1:22). The Lord protects him from foul language and angry responses (Col. 3:8). He is a man of integrity. He is considerate, sensitive and reflects the love of God. The Lord draws him one step closer to Himself each day. He is a leader and will be a great father to his children. He is an unselfish man who loves my daughter as Christ loves the Church. He sees challenges as opportunities and uncertainty as avenues to deeper faith. He is a hard worker, a man of strength and integrity. They will marry at the time God has set for them to marry. Wherever he is and whatever his circumstances, the peace of God rules in his heart, mind, and situation (Colossians 3:15). He is strong, loving, kind and wise. This is my prayer and declaration in Jesus' name.

PRAY FOR CHILDREN OF THE WORLD:

They will find a lifelong companion who loves Jesus and seeks Christ and His Kingdom first.

DECLARATIONS AGAINST SIBLING RIVALRY

It is sometimes hard for siblings to get along with one another. In most cases, sibling rivalry is rooted in jealousy or competition. In the story of Cain and Abel, their rivalry went further than a few arguments where Cain murdered his brother. Cain was angry and jealous because God had accepted Abel's offering but not Cain's; therefore, Cain had a fit of all-consuming jealousy against his brother, which led to him committing murder. Although God warned Cain about sin, his jealousy led to anger and harmful feelings, eventually leading to murder. He could not overcome the temptation of sin.

It is not uncommon for older siblings to desire to be more dominant over their younger siblings. Regarding Jacob and Esau, the older sibling would serve Jacob, as Jacob was the chosen one. Although God chose Jacob for future rulership, their father, Isaac, decided to bless Esau instead and Jacob's mother arranged for Jacob to receive the blessing by deceit. It is evident that Esau was his father's favourite. Both parents didn't help make sure the brothers got along in this situation. The cause of sibling rivalry can be overcome by respect, kindness and love. God desires that siblings live in harmony and love with each other. *"Behold, how good and how pleasant it is for brethren to dwell together in unity!"* *(Ps. 133:1).*

Words of Wisdom: As parents, we have a role to play in tempering sibling rivalry. Our job is to raise our children to be Christlike. We must take care not to fuel the fire of sibling rivalry. We need to show unconditional love, not always be so concerned, and show favouritism towards one child. We must teach our children to honour one another and insist that they treat each other with respect, kindness and love, and we should also do the same. Family love needs to be unconditional.

Scripture Meditation: Ephesians 4:31–32

"Let all bitterness and wrath and anger and clamour [perpetual animosity, resentment, strife, fault-finding] and slander be put away from you, along with every kind of malice [all spitefulness, verbal abuse, malevolence]. Be kind and helpful to one another, tender-hearted [compassionate, understanding], forgiving one another [readily and freely], just as God in Christ also forgave you."

1 Corinthians 13:4-7 - "Love suffers long and is kind; love does not envy; love does not parade itself, is not puffed up; does not behave rudely, does not seek its own, is not provoked, thinks no evil; does not rejoice in iniquity, but rejoices in the truth; bears all things, believes all things, hopes all things, endures all things."

Your Declaration: I declare that my children are God's chosen vessels. They put on a heart of compassion, kindness, humility, gentleness, and patience. They bear graciously with one another and willingly forgive each other (Col. 3:13). Above all these, they put on unselfish love, the perfect bond of unity. They seek the best in each other. Unforgiveness, envy, jealousy and offence will not take over their hearts. I come against all forms of division and plead the blood of Jesus against strife, division and misunderstanding. The peace of Christ is the controlling factor in my children's hearts (Col. 3:15). My family live in unity and harmony. The love of God overflows in our lives. I break the hold and power of discord and strife in my family and rebuke the devil's plans to divide us. We overcome challenges together through the power of prayer. My children are humble and treat each other with respect. They help each other with cheerful hearts. They accept corrections and are willing to change their ways. They support each other in good and bad times and show compassion. They do not act strange to each other but are full of love and kindness. Our home overflows with God's love, unity, kindness and peace. Lord, I dedicate my family to you. The grace of Jesus Christ our Lord and the sweet fellowship of the Holy Spirit keeps my children united always and forever. This is my prayer and declaration in Jesus' name.

PRAY FOR CHILDREN OF THE WORLD:
Pray that they are humble and treat each other with respect. They help each other with cheerful hearts and are willing to change their ways.

DECLARATIONS AGAINST ANGER

"Know this, my beloved brothers: let every person be quick to hear, slow to speak, slow to anger; for the anger of man does not produce the righteousness of God." (James 1:19-20)

We all get angry sometimes—it's a natural reaction to certain situations. However, when we are angry and lose control, we hurt other people. Anger has an impact on our lives as well as the lives of others. When we speak out of anger, the words leave behind scars that we cannot remove, no matter how many times we apologise. If we learn to control our anger and teach our children how Jesus taught and modelled, we will discover that we are living in God's peace more and more.

When children are angry and out of control, it isn't easy to act reasonably. Excessive or chronic anger will always have negative, self-destructive consequences, both for the one who is angry and for the people around them. Jesus is our best moral teacher on how to deal with anger. He cares about each child and understands anger. He understands how to deal with being criticised or mistreated. I pray God will give your children obedient hearts and convict them of wrongdoing. May He help them understand the root cause of their rebellion so you will know how to pray and deal with it. I pray the Lord will help your children deal with the source of their frustration and anger without taking it out on other family members and friends. Parents, please also remember that God forbids us from provoking our children to anger. *"Fathers, do not provoke your children to anger, but bring them up in the discipline and instruction of the Lord." (Ephesians 6:4 ESV)*

Words of Wisdom: If you are dealing with a difficult and angry child, God will give you the strength to deal with the situation and overcome their behaviour. Ask God to grant you the patience you will need as you assist him/her in becoming a better child. Ask for discernment as to what is causing the children's negative behaviour, so you can address the right issue and thank Him for His guidance. Let us also pray for ourselves as parents, asking God to keep us from provoking our children. We may unknowingly provoke our children's anger in various subtle ways. Instead, we should show kindness and consideration. Look for ways you might be making your children angry. What you find might surprise you! May God give us daily grace to raise our children in Godly discipline and instruction in Jesus' name.

Scripture Meditation: Proverbs 14:29
"He who is slow to anger has great understanding [and profits from his self-control], but he who is quick-tempered exposes and exalts his foolishness [for all to see]."

Your Declaration: I declare that my children are slow to speak, quick to hear, and slow to anger (James 1:19). They avoid bitterness, anger, malice, slander, strife, jealousy, envy and evil speaking (Eph. 4:31). No corrupt words will come out of their mouths, only words that are good for edification and will give grace to those who hear them. The Lord gives them grace and strength, and they no longer fulfil the desires of the flesh. They will not grieve the Holy Spirit of God, by whom they were sealed for the day of redemption (Eph. 4:29, 30). Anger and rage will not consume them. They have the peace of God and will not allow others to get them angry. They cease from anger and forsake wrath (Ps. 37:8). When they are upset, troubled and disturbed, the Lord grants them peace in the midst of the storm. Their heart is cleansed from all bitterness and anger. The peace of Christ rules in their hearts at all times (Col. 3:15). They are kind, tenderhearted, and forgiving, even as God in Christ forgave them (Eph. 4:32). This is my prayer and declaration in Jesus' name.

PRAY FOR CHILDREN OF THE WORLD:

Pray that they cease from anger, and forsake wrath.

- WEEK 47 –

DECLARATIONS
OVER SPORTS ACTIVITIES

Every week, thousands of youngsters around the world participate in sports. 55.2% of young adults in the UK participate in at least one sports session every week, and this figure rises to 86.6% among 11-16 year olds! Sports are an essential aspect of God's creation, a gift to be enjoyed for the glory of God. It is a part of life that can be given to God as an act of worship. It will make a significant difference when our youngsters understand that their sport can be offered to God as an act of worship!

Many parents recognise the need to instil the value of good sportsmanship in their children from an early age. The excitement your children feel when they participate in sports is not beyond the comprehension of God. He is not removed from the highs and lows experienced throughout the competition. As parents, your heartbeat is God's heartbeat, and your happiness is God's delight. He is the one who gave our children the ability to play sports, after all. So, do any of your children participate in any sports? I pray that they will give it their all, play fairly, and play to the glory of God; after all, they are participating in worship. They will not use their gifts to seek fame but glorify God. In the name of Jesus, none of their bones will be broken on the field of play. The Lord will protect your children physically, spiritually, mentally, and emotionally as they participate in their favourite sports.

Words of Wisdom: There are many risks associated with playing sports, so we cannot afford to be slack when praying for our children. I have declared Psalm 34:20 over my child numerous times while he has participated in sports. When you pray for your child, you should begin by praising the Father, worshipping Him, and expressing appreciation to Him for giving you such a talented child. Assume your position as the authority in the fight against anxiety, fear, and discouragement whilst praying for your child's heart to be at peace. It is not always the case that they bring the victory back home. In times of disappointment, pray that the Lord would strengthen your child and give them the power to triumph over adverse circumstances, not harbour any ill thoughts towards anyone, and keep their hearts pure. I pray the Lord will help your child maintain a pleasant and godly demeanour while competing in sports and be polite to their coaches and kind to their teammates.

Scripture Meditation: 1 Corinthians 9:24-25 (AMP)
"Do you not know that in a race all the runners run [their very best to win], but only one receives the prize? Run [your race] in such a way that you may seize the prize and make it yours! Now every athlete who [goes into training and] competes in the games is disciplined and exercises self-control in all things. They do it to win a crown that withers, but we [do it to receive] an imperishable [crown that cannot wither]."

Your Declaration: I declare that my children are safe in all their sports activities. They are kept free from injuries. The Lord protects all their bones; not one of them will be broken (Ps.

34:20). The Lord rescues my children from every trap and protects them from deadly opponents. He keeps them from the hands of the wicked and protects them from violent men who intend to trip up their steps (Ps. 140:4). The Lord gives them all the strength they need to be a champion in their chosen field. They find favour with their coaches and other mates. They play for God's glory for the good of their team. They conduct themselves in a God-pleasing manner and show good sportsmanship despite the outcome. They have a body which is fit and strong. They play with a good heart but never lose heart. Their workouts and the games they play are blessed, and those with whom they exercise or compete are blessed. The Lord defends my children against injury and sends His Spirit to protect and guide them. They are protected from physical harm and play to their best. They prosper in all their sports activities and will be in good health even as their soul prospers (3 John: 2). They will not indulge in things which will make them less fit than they ought to be. My children will always have healthy bodies and healthy minds. They have strength, endurance, courage and agility as they compete or train. The Lord God will be a wall of fire around them (protecting them from enemies), and He will be the glory in their midst (Zech. 2:5). The Lord makes my children's feet like the feet of a deer and enables them to stand on heights (Ps. 18:33). He gives them His shield of victory, and His right hand sustains them. You, Lord, make my children great. You broaden the path beneath them so that their ankles do not turn. Thank you for all the talent you have given my children. This is my prayer and declaration in Jesus' name.

PRAY FOR CHILDREN OF THE WORLD:

Pray that they have a healthy body, a healthy mind, and they are protected from physical harm.

DECLARATIONS
FOR CREATIVITY

Did you know your children are creative? Everyone is! You, your family, and many others have been blessed with wonderful creative abilities because God made us creative just like He is. He made your family unique and loaded your children with special gifts on entry into the world. None of them came into the world empty. He is the Giver of all creative gifts, the Supreme Creator who made us in His image. *"So God created man in His own image; in the image of God He created him; male and female He created them" (Gen. 1:27).* We are a reflection of Him, and He wants us to use our creativity to make the world a better place. *"You are worthy, O Lord, to receive glory and honour and power; for You created all things, and by Your will they exist and were created" (Rev. 4:11).* Our Creator has endowed us with specialties in differing areas, just as He has given each member of the Body of Christ gifts of the Spirit. So, likewise, he has given each of us gifts of creativity. Your children have creativity in areas God has given them for particular purposes; as always, they are for His glory.

"And Moses said to the children of Israel, "See, the Lord has called by name Bezalel the son of Uri, the son of Hur, of the tribe of Judah; and He has filled him with the Spirit of God, in wisdom and understanding, in knowledge and all manner of workmanship, to design artistic works, to work in gold and silver and bronze, in

cutting jewels for setting, in carving wood, and to work in all manner of artistic workmanship. And He has put in his heart the ability to teach, in him and Aholiab the son of Ahisamach, of the tribe of Dan. He has filled them with skill to do all manner of work of the engraver and the designer and the tapestry maker, in blue, purple, and scarlet thread, and fine linen, and of the weaver— those who do every work and those who design artistic works" (Exod. 35:30-35)

Bezalel was filled with the Spirit of God's creative abilities. God filled him with skill, intelligence, knowledge, and all craftsmanship. He was given unique talents and abilities to work creatively on the construction of the tabernacle of God, and he was also inspired to teach these to others. I pray your children will be filled with the Spirit of God's creative abilities in the name of Jesus.

Words of Wisdom: The Lord gave Bezalel these creative gifts to utilize for His glory and be a blessing to others. We are to be His working in the lives of others. God created our children to glorify Him in good works. Their talents and abilities are to be used for the glory of God. A buried talent is useless, but a skill that is utilized displays the glory of God, who gives all our children those special abilities, talents, and creative skills. "Do you see a man skillful in his work? He will stand before kings; he will not stand before obscure men (Prov. 22:29)."

Scripture Meditation: 1 Timothy 4:14-15
"Do not neglect the gift that is in you, which was given to you by prophecy with the laying on of the hands of the eldership. Meditate

on these things; give yourself entirely to them, that your progress may be evident to all."

Your Declaration: I declare that my children are creative for the glory of God. They are fearfully and wonderfully made (Ps. 139:14). They were created in the image and after the likeness of a creative God (Gen. 1:27). The DNA of God's creative power is in them. My children develop, grow, reproduce and multiply in creativity. God has deposited His Spirit of excellence, wisdom, insight and creativity inside them. They are created to be creative, birth new ideas, and bring hidden gems into existence. They will use their imagination to bring about positive change in the world. God has filled them with wisdom and skill, intelligence and understanding, and knowledge in all workmanship (Exod. 35:31). He has put in their hearts the ability to teach others (Exod. 35:34). They will bless the Lord and bring much more than enough for the service of the Kingdom. They come up with new ideas and bring solutions to problems around them, their community, and their nation. This is my prayer and declaration in Jesus' name.

PRAY FOR CHILDREN OF THE WORLD:

Pray that God will fill them with wisdom and skill, intelligence, understanding and knowledge in all manner of workmanship.

DECLARATIONS OVER THE EYE GATE, MOUTH GATE & EAR GATE

"Keep your heart with all diligence, for out of it spring the issues of life. Put away from you a deceitful mouth, and put perverse lips far from you. Let your eyes look straight ahead, and your eyelids look right before you." (Prov. 4:23-25)

Our children have three primary gates through which they receive and process information. The things they allow into those gateways directly affect the spiritual condition of their heart. We all have an ear, an eye, and a mouth gate. Whether or not your children walk in the Spirit or the flesh depends on what they let into their gateways. We can open the gates to the things that edify our spirits and enhance our being filled with the Holy Spirit, or we can let in things that grieve the Holy Spirit and hinder our ability to walk in the Spirit. These gates are entries through which negative influences can enter. Protecting the gates is essential because our ears, eyes and mouth are gateways to our hearts. Taking charge of these gateways is crucial to walking in the Spirit and having victory over the flesh.

These are three gates that lead to the soul:

The Eye-Gate (What you see): Jesus said of the eye-gate: *"Your eye is like a lamp that provides light for your body. When your eye is healthy, your whole body is filled with light. But when your eye* is unhealthy, your whole body is filled with darkness. And if the light you think you have is actually darkness, how deep that darkness is!" (Matt. 6:22-23 NLT). Without a doubt, the Lord is telling us that to guard the eye-gate is key to walking in the Spirit where our soul is "filled with light." If the eye is healthy, it gives light to the entire body. Your child's eye is the lamp to their body. Once this gateway is defiled, a strong spirit of pornography, lust, etc., can enter. Our eyes function much like the lens of a camera; they take an image and transmit that picture to our spirit. Therefore, we must be cautious about what we allow our children to see on TV, mobile phones, iPads, and other devices. The enemy can use all of these to defile their eye gate.

The Mouth-Gate (What you say): The Bible speaks of the mouth-gate: *"Put away from you a deceitful (lying, misleading) mouth, and put devious lips far from you." (Prov. 4:24 AMP)*. The more we take charge of our tongue, the more we will enjoy the presence of the Spirit of God because "Death and life are in the power of the tongue!" (Prov. 18:21). Beware of the idle words you speak over yourself, your children and others. Controlling your tongue is essential to walking in the Spirit. It is important to remember that you should not use the same tongue to say praises one minute and curses the next. Our words hold power. We must teach our children to think before they speak. Children imitate what they see and repeat what they hear!

The Ear-Gate (What you hear): *"So then faith comes by hearing, and hearing by the word of God." (Romans 10:17)*. God gave us eyelids to shut out what we don't want to see, but He didn't give us earlids, so we must encourage our children to walk away from things they shouldn't listen to lest they quench the Spirit of God. Listening to the wrong thing will affect your child's hearing gateway.

Are you aware of the music that your children listen to regularly? Some parents are unaware of how sexually explicit lyrics in popular music might influence their children's development. Are you aware that sexual references in music lyrics are becoming more popular? Devices such as Mobile phones, iPods, MP4 players, and lightweight earphones are used to deliver this music privately and discretely to your youngster. If you don't know what your child is listening to, how can you determine whether or not there is a problem? Is he or she participating in online games that feature visually violent content and filthy language? A young person's behaviour can change as a result of this, and they may turn violent as a result. If it's dirty, encourage them to walk away. If it's gossip, they should walk away. If it's profanity, ask them to walk away. If it's blasphemous, they should walk away. Finally, tell them to walk away if they sense the Spirit grieved in them. When a child's hearing gateway is defiled, it is hard for them to hear the truth of God's word.

Words of Wisdom: Please encourage your children to guard their eye, ear and mouth gates. This will significantly strengthen their walk in the Spirit. Pray and ask God to protect these gateways into your children's lives and stop anything unclean from entering (2 Chronicles 23:19). Pray with your children, teach them to know, meditate upon and understand God's word. Regularly, anoint them with oil. Take authority, command any strongholds in your children's lives to be destroyed through the power of the

Holy Spirit and plead the blood of Jesus on their eye, mouth and ear gates. God's desire is for your children's ears, eyes, and hearts to be filled to overflowing with the gracious words and presence of Jesus. No weapon fashioned against your family shall prosper in the name of Jesus!

Scripture Meditation: Matthew 6:22-23 (AMP)

"The eye is the lamp of the body; so if your eye is clear [spiritually perceptive], your whole body will be full of light [benefiting from God's precepts]. But if your eye is bad [spiritually blind], your whole body will be full of darkness [devoid of God's precepts]. So if the [very] light inside you [your inner self, your heart, your conscience] is darkness, how great and terrible is that darkness!"

Your Declaration: I declare that the Lord sets a guard over my children's mouths. He keeps watching over the door of their lips (Ps. 141:3). The eye of their heart is enlightened, so they know the hope to which God has called them, the riches of His glorious inheritance in the saints (Eph. 1:18). I plead the blood of Jesus over my children's eyes, mouths and ear gates. They are conscious of what they watch and hear regularly. They make Godly choices about what they allow into their eye and ear gates and what comes out of their mouths. They guard all the gateways into their soul, for in doing so, they guard their heart, and then they can guard their mouth. My children set no worthless or wicked thing before their eyes. They will not know wickedness in the name of Jesus (Ps. 101:3-4). I speak Joshua 1:8 that this Book of the law (The Bible) shall not depart from my children's mouth; but they shall meditate in it day and night, that they may observe to do according to all that is written in it. Then they will make their way prosperous and will have good success. My children are quick to listen, slow to speak, and slow to anger (James 1:19). They keep their tongue from evil and their lips from speaking lies (Ps. 34:13). Their mouth will speak truth, and wickedness is repulsive and loathsome to their lips. All the words of their mouth are in righteousness (upright, in right standing with God); there is nothing contrary to truth or perverted (crooked) in them (Prov. 8:7-8). They give attention to God's Word and incline their ears to His sayings. This is my prayer and declaration in Jesus' name.

PRAY FOR CHILDREN OF THE WORLD:

They keep their tongue from evil and their lips from speaking lies.

- WEEK 50 -

DECLARATIONS
LIVING IN THE WORD

The Bible, God's Word, has the power to change a person completely. It helps us fight and resist sin, which easily entangles us. *"For the Word of God is alive and powerful, and sharper than any two-edged sword, penetrating even to the division of soul and spirit, and joints and marrow, and is a discerner of the thoughts and intents of the heart" (Heb. 4:12)*. God's Word is powerful because it gives us all the answers we need to live a holy life. It is the path that leads to spiritual growth. As Christians, we are responsible for leading lives pleasing to God and bringing glory to Him. Sin is something that God hates, and he wants us to feel the same way about it. When our children feed on God's Word, they experience spiritual growth. Their faith will increase and progress toward a more intimate relationship with God.

"As newborn babes, desire the pure milk of the word, that you may grow thereby" (1 Peter 2:2).

Newborn infants do not need their parents' money; they do not require a car or a college scholarship. A newborn infant requires milk. God calls our families to seek His Word and rely on it to survive and grow in this world, just as a newborn infant relies on breast milk. *"Let the word of Christ dwell in you richly in all wisdom, teaching and admonishing one another in psalms and hymns and spiritual songs, singing with grace in your hearts to the*

Lord" *(Colossians 3:16)*. The Bible is the cornerstone of our children's spiritual development. *"Your word is a lamp to my feet and a light to my path" (Psalm 119:105).*

Words of Wisdom: The Word of God is the most powerful weapon our children have at their disposal to combat the enemy. When Jesus responded to Satan in Matthew 4:4, *"Man shall not live by bread alone, but by every Word that comes from the mouth of God,"* He did so because He understood the importance of the written Word. He had memorised God's Word and used it in his hour of weakness when Satan tried to tempt him. He had been in the wilderness for 40 days and nights, and his stomach grumbled with hunger. During that very moment, the devil approached Jesus and said, "If you are the Son of God, command that these stones become bread" (Matt. 4:3). Those who have the Word committed to memory can defeat Satan at any time, even at their most vulnerable moments. Therefore, we must teach our children to commit God's Word to memory if we want them to be able to resist temptation and live victorious lives. The Holy Spirit will bring it to their minds at the appropriate time.

Scripture Meditation: Psalm 1:1-3 (AMP)
"Blessed [fortunate, prosperous, and favoured by God] is the man who does not walk in the counsel of the wicked [following their advice and example], nor stand in the path of sinners, nor sit [down to rest] in the seat of scoffers (ridiculers). But his delight is in the law of the Lord, and on His law [His precepts and teachings] he [habitually] meditates day and night. And he will be like a tree firmly planted [and fed] by streams of water, which yields its fruit in its season; its leaf does not wither; and in whatever he does, he

prospers [and comes to maturity]."

Your Declaration: I declare that the Spirit of the Sovereign Lord is on my children. The Lord has anointed them to proclaim good news to the poor. He has sent them to heal the broken-hearted, to proclaim freedom to the captives and release from darkness the prisoners who are bound (Isaiah 61:1). My family delight in the law of the Lord and meditate on His law day and night (Ps. 1:2). Whatever we do shall prosper in the name of Jesus. My children treasure the Word of God and store it in their hearts so that they may not sin against Him (Ps 119:11). They keep His testimonies and seek God with their whole heart (Ps 119: 2). They walk in the law of the LORD and hear the voice of their Good Shepherd. They will not hear the voice of a stranger in the name of Jesus. The Word of God dwells in my family richly. We seek first the Kingdom of God and His righteousness, and all things are added unto us (Matt. 6:33). We are imitators of God (Eph. 5:1). Jesus is the author and developer of our faith. My children will not wander from God's commandments (Ps 119: 10). They delight themselves in God's statutes and will not forget His Word (Ps 119:16). This is my prayer and declaration in Jesus' name.

PRAY FOR CHILDREN OF THE WORLD:

That they seek the Lord and long for Him with all their heart.

DECLARATIONS
TO SPEAK THE WORD

God's Word is alive and active. It lives and gives life. It possesses an unstoppable supernatural ability to do what He chooses. When spoken in the name of Jesus, the Word of God has amazing power to overcome insurmountable problems. The Bible states in Isaiah 55:11, *"So will My word be which goes out of My mouth; it will not return to Me void (useless, without result), without accomplishing what I desire, and without succeeding in the matter for which I sent it"*. God's Word will not come back to Him void. When we proclaim God's Word, we tap into boundless power! As we consistently proclaim God's Word and encourage our children to do the same, all kinds of good things will begin to happen, and breakthroughs will manifest in Jesus' name. We must teach our children to stand boldly on God's Word, encourage them to speak the Word, and expect its boundless power to produce miraculous results in their lives.

Words of Wisdom: Jesus said, *"It is written,"* to the devil three times, and the enemy's plans were defeated! It is essential to encourage our children to speak God's Word confidently. Words have power when spoken in faith and when they are the Word of God spoken through our mouths. We should follow Jesus' example and quote the scriptures. The Bible says in Jeremiah 23:28-29, "Let the one who has my word speak it faithfully..." "Is not my word like fire," declares the LORD, "and like a hammer that breaks a rock in pieces?" When our children speak the Word of God, they are tapping into limitless power!

Scripture Meditation: Isaiah 59:21 (AMP)

"As for Me, this is My covenant with them," says the Lord: "My Spirit which is upon you [writing the law of God on the heart], and My words which I have put in your mouth shall not depart from your mouth, nor from the mouths of your [true, spiritual] children, nor from the mouth of your children's children," says the Lord, "from now and forever.""

Your Declaration: I declare that my children's mouth will not transgress (Ps 17:3). By the Word of God's lips they are kept away from the paths of the destroyer (Ps 17:4). Their words are Holy Spirit anointed, for Christ dwells in their words. They will not allow any corrupt communication to proceed out of their mouth. Instead, they will speak only that which is good, full of grace and edifying to others (Ephesians 4:29). Their heart is overflowing with a good theme. Their tongue is the pen of a ready writer (Ps. 45:1). Their mouth speaks wisdom, and their tongue talks of justice. The law of God is in their heart; none of their steps shall slide in the name of Jesus (Psalm 37:30-31). My children speak only what they hear our Father say, setting a watch before their lips that they might not sin against Him. Their thoughts and speech are guided by God's Word. I speak God's covenant in Isaiah 59:21 over them: "My Spirit who is upon you, and My words which I have put in your mouth, shall not depart from your mouth, nor from the mouth of your descendants, nor from the mouth of your descendants' descendants," says the Lord, "from this time and forevermore". I therefore declare: The Spirit of God that is upon my children and His words which He has put in their mouth, shall not depart from their mouth, nor from the mouths of their children, nor from the mouths of their children's children from now and forever. This is my prayer and declaration in Jesus' name.

PRAY FOR CHILDREN OF THE WORLD:

Pray that thy are kept away from the paths of the destroyer.

PLEADING THE BLOOD OF JESUS

The blood of Jesus is powerful. Satan fears the blood of Jesus! Whatever you may be dealing with, I pray that God's peace will envelop and sustain you. Put your trust in Him and confess this powerful prayer:

Confession:

Father, in the name of Jesus, I plead the blood of Jesus on my entire family. I apply the blood of Jesus as a hedge of protection around my children (name them). I plead the blood of Jesus on our physical bodies, souls, and spirit. I plead the blood of Jesus against any demons that may try and come against us. I bind every assignment of the enemy and plead the blood of Jesus against agents of Satan that may try and come against us. I plead the blood of Jesus against any counter-attacks sent against us. I cover my family and my home with the blood of Jesus. I cover our jobs, offices, my children's school, college/university and all our cars and possessions with the blood of Jesus. I cover our finances with the blood of Jesus. I cover our minds with the blood of Jesus. No weapon formed against us shall prosper. Great shall be the peace of my family in the name of Jesus.

I plead the blood of Jesus against any natural accidents or catastrophes that may come against me or any family member. I plead the blood of Jesus against any diseases, illnesses or sicknesses that could come against us. I plead the protection that is in the Name of Jesus upon my family. We shall not die, but live and declare the works of the Lord. I plead the blood of Jesus against sudden premature death. None of us shall die in our sleep. I cover our dreams with the blood of Jesus. We shall not mourn in Jesus' Name.

Father, in the name of Jesus, I have complete faith and believe that the Blood of Jesus will now protect my family against all the things I have just pled His blood on.

Thank you Father, thank you Jesus, thank you Holy Spirit. In Jesus Mighty Name I pray. Amen.

> *"And when I see the blood, I will pass over you;*
> *And the plague shall not be on you to destroy you..."*
> *(Exodus 12:13)*

DECLARATIONS DURING BEREAVEMENT

Are you mourning the loss of a friend or family? Are your children in agony due to the loss of a loved one? The loss of family is never easy. Every death brings a loss, and every loss is accompanied by pain. Grieving can be the most challenging time for families. I've been through it myself, and it is a harrowing season to go through. Losing a parent, sibling, friend or close relative is a tragedy when one is still young. However, if these feelings are affecting your children, there are things you can try that may help. First, relying upon your family, friends, and faith is essential for support through difficult times. The Bible reminds us that God will always be by our side to comfort us, renew our hope, and provide guidance in good and challenging times. The Bible states in Psalm 34:18-19, *"The Lord is near to the broken-hearted and saves the crushed in spirit. Many are the afflictions of the righteous, but the LORD delivers him out of them all."* This is a reassurance that God is always with your family, even when you feel alone. When you don't think God is there, He is still keeping an eye on you and your family. When you may not believe God is near, He is still watching over you and your children.

"I am with you and will watch over you wherever you go, and I will bring you back to this land. I will not leave you until I have done what I have promised you." (Genesis 28:15)

Grief may seem never-ending; believe me, I've been there, yet, you will eventually find consolation by listening to God's Word and allowing yourself time to process. You will feel joy again, even if it doesn't feel like it now. The Lord is watching over you and your children. He uses the grieving process to bring us back to wholeness. It is a necessary part of our healing. I strongly encourage you to invite Jesus into your suffering. He is right there with you in your pain. *"Surely He has borne our griefs and carried our sorrows...He was wounded for our transgressions, He was bruised for our iniquities; the chastisement for our peace was upon Him, and by His stripes we are healed"* (Isaiah 53:4-5).

Words of Wisdom: Give your children the space and time to grieve, encourage them to be open and honest about their emotions, and assure them that they are not alone in their loss. Grief is a normal part of life; it takes time to recover. Read Bible scriptures together, pray with them and speak God's Word over your children. In scripture, we can find ease and consolation as we battle to overcome loss as a family. The encouraging news is that God will never leave us alone in our grief; He will always provide us with love and hope. Matthew 5:4 *"Blessed are those who mourn, for they shall be comforted."* In this time, don't be scared to rely on others. In your loss, you and your children are not alone. Others have experienced the same waves of grief, sadness, and hope as we have. May the Lord strengthen you and your family in difficult and lonely times.

Scripture Meditation: 1 Thessalonians 4:13-18 (AMP)
"Now we do not want you to be uninformed, believers, about those who are asleep [in death], so that you will not grieve [for them] as

the others do who have no hope [beyond this present life]. For if we believe that Jesus died and rose again [as in fact He did], even so God [in this same way—by raising them from the dead] will bring with Him those [believers] who have fallen asleep in Jesus. For we say this to you by the Lord's [own] word, that we who are still alive and remain until the coming of the Lord, will in no way precede [into His presence] those [believers] who have fallen asleep [in death]. For the Lord Himself will come down from heaven with a shout of command, with the voice of the archangel and with the [blast of the] trumpet of God, and the dead in Christ will rise first. Then we who are alive and remain [on the earth] will simultaneously be caught up (raptured) together with them [the resurrected ones] in the clouds to meet the Lord in the air, and so we will always be with the Lord! Therefore comfort and encourage one another with these words [concerning our reunion with believers who have died]."

Your Declaration: I declare for my children and myself that God makes everything new. He shall wipe away all tears from our eyes; and there shall be no more death in my family, neither sorrow, nor crying, neither shall there be any more pain in our home (Rev. 21:4). Our hearts will rejoice once more, and no one will be able to take that joy away from us. Who else except you, Lord, do we have in heaven? And there is none upon earth that we desire besides you. Our flesh and hearts may fail in this time of grief, but God, you are the strength of our hearts and our portion forever (Ps. 73:25-26). You, Lord Jesus, were a man of sorrows and acquainted with grief; surely you have borne our griefs and carried our sorrows. You were wounded for our transgressions, bruised as a result of our sins; the chastisement for our peace was upon you, and it is by your stripes that we have been healed

(Isa. 53:4-5). Heal and strengthen our hearts, Lord. Give us the grace to move through this difficult time of loss and fill us with your joy and peace. Draw my family closer to you, be more dependent on you and seek you daily. My children shall fear nothing because the Lord is with them; He is our God. The Lord will strengthen and help us. He will uphold us with His righteous right hand, a hand of justice, power, victory, and salvation (Isa. 41:10). We will not be afraid, nor will we be terrified, for terror will not come near us. We will not be worried or terrified by anything. Though we walk through the valley of the shadow of death, we will fear no evil; for you are with us; your rod and your staff, they comfort us through this difficult time of grief. All my children will be taught by the Lord, and their peace and well-being will be abundant. They shall be established in righteousness and far from oppression. Anyone who gathers against my family will fall for our sake (Isa. 54:13-15). When my children pass through the waters, the Lord will be with them; and through the rivers, they will not be overwhelmed. When my family walk through the fire, we will not be scorched. The flame will not burn us (Isa. 43:2). Praise be to the God and Father of our Lord Jesus Christ, the Father of compassion and all comfort, who comforts us in all our sorrows so that we can comfort those who are in distress with the consolation we receive from God. (2 Cor. 1:3-4). This God is our God forever and ever; He will be our guide even to the end (Ps. 48:14). This is my prayer and declaration in Jesus' name.

PRAY FOR CHILDREN OF THE WORLD:
Pray the Angel of the Lord will encamp around them and protect each of them from sudden death and calamity.

Steps to Peace with God

God loves you and desires that you have peace in this life and in the life to come. *"We have peace with God through our Lord Jesus Christ"* (Romans 5:1).

Because Jesus Christ, our Lord, is the only way for us to experience peace, abundance, and eternal life, I would like to encourage you to confess the prayer below if you do not know Jesus Christ as your personal Lord and Saviour. May the peace of our Lord Jesus Christ abide with you now and forever. Amen.

PRAYER

How to Pray:

Dear Lord Jesus, I know that I am a sinner, and ask for Your forgiveness. I repent of all my sins. I believe You died for my sins and rose from the dead. I turn from my sins and invite You to come into my heart and life. Be the Lord of my heart. I ask Your Holy Spirit to come into my life. I want to trust and follow You as my Lord and Saviour now and for ever. In Your Name. Amen.

God's Assurance is His Word
If you prayed this prayer, the Bible says ...
"Everyone who calls on the name of the Lord will be saved."
—Romans 10:13

ABOUT THE AUTHOR

Freda Lade-Ajumobi was born in Manchester, England. She is a graduate of Art and Design and attended the History Maker's Bible School at Emmanuel Centre, Victoria, London, UK.

She is an anointed Minister, author, speaker and a teacher of the word of God. A prayer warrior and an intercessor with a passion for serving. She has been serving the Body of Christ for over 35 years and gave her life to Christ in 1984.

She is the Pastor of Church of New Destiny UK. The founder and leader of Praying Parents® UK, Warriors of God (A Global intercessory Ministry touching Nations), and Destiny Changers.

Her calling and anointing is in the area of the prophetic, encouragement and teaching of the Word and has enriched many lives with this gift. She is the founder of Unique Ministries, a ministry that is fulfilling the call of God on her life, to teach, preach, inspire, encourage and minister to the body of Christ across all denominations.

She is married and blessed with a lovely family.

She loves the Lord with all her heart and desires above all to spread the knowledge of God's glory to the uttermost ends of the earth through her books, Internet blogs, paintings and ministering the Word of God to a hurt and broken world.

MORE FROM FREDA LADE-AJUMOBI
Find on Amazon

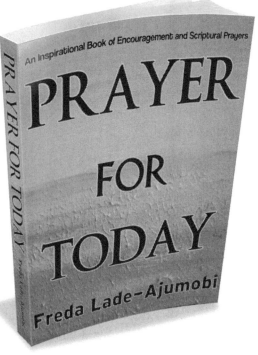

You can use PRAYER for TODAY as a devotional or buy it as a gift for a loved one or anyone you think would need some encouragement and prayers.

- **ISBN-10** : 1490567755
- **ISBN-13** : 978-1490567754

Reviewed on Amazon:

"This is a very powerful, easy to read book with great prayer points that yield results. Pastor Lade is truly an anointed, gifted woman of God."

https://www.amazon.co.uk/Prayer-Today

Contact us: www.prayingparents.co.uk

ALSO AVAILABLE AS E-BOOK:
Find on Amazon

https://www.amazon.co.uk/PRAYER-TODAY-Freda-Lade-Ajumobi-ebook/

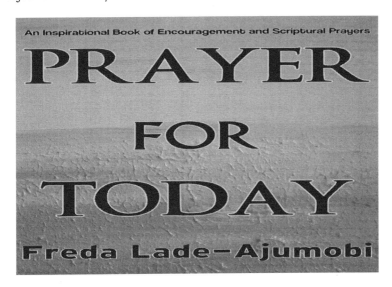

- **ASIN** : B00CEOJHCC

Printed in Great Britain
by Amazon

87179249R00122